Super
Paper
Airplanes

Super Paper Airplanes

Biplanes to Space Planes

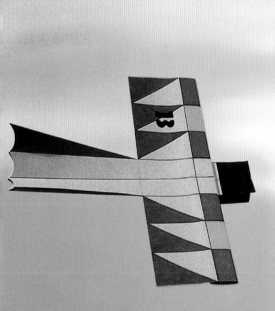

Norman Schmidt

Sterling Publishing Co., Inc.   New York
A Sterling/Tamos Book

A Sterling/Tamos Book

Published in 2002 by Sterling Publishing Company, Inc.
387 Park Avenue South, New York, NY 10016

TAMOS Books Inc.
300 Wales Avenue, Winnipeg, MB, Canada R2M 2S9

10   9   8   7   6   5   4   3   2   1

Distributed in Canada by Sterling Publishing Co., Inc.
c/o Canadian Manda Group, 1 Atlantic Avenue, Suite 105
Toronto, Ontario, Canada M6K 3E7
Distributed in Great Britain and Europe by Chris Lloyd at Orca
Book Services, Stanley House, Fleets Lane, Poole BH15 3AJ,
England
Distributed in Australia by Capricorn Link (Australia) Pty Ltd.
P.O. Box 704, Windsor, NSW 2756, Australia

Design   Norman Schmidt
Photography   Jerry Grajewski & Walter Kaiser,
                Custom Images, Ltd.

Printed and bound in China
All rights reserved

ISBN 1-895569-47-8

Contents

Flight

People have been obsessed with the idea of flight ever since they looked into the sky and saw birds soaring gently overhead. Mythical stories in many cultures around the world have flying creatures of all sorts, including human beings. When did the reality of human flight begin?

Archeologists in Egypt have discovered a small wooden bird, carved from lightweight sycamore wood, that has a very aerodynamic shape. This small wooden bird is unlike any real bird because its tail has both horizontal and vertical surfaces, just like present-day airplanes. It is not known whether this was a toy, a weather vane, or a small model of some larger craft.

There are other examples of flying toys, such as the Saqqara bird invented by the Greek philosopher Archytas in about 345 B.C. It was a small wooden dove attached to an arm that allowed it to "lift off" in wavering flight. It is not known how the bird was propelled. At about the same time the Chinese philosopher Mo Tzu constructed what was possibly the first kite, which is simply a tethered airplane. Some Europeans made wings of wood, cloth, and bird feathers, strapped them to their arms, and jumped off high buildings. In 1020 Eilmer "the flying monk" did this, and attained some success with flight, but broke both his legs in the attempt. In the 1500s the artist and inventor, Leonardo da Vinci, made many drawings and models of different kinds of aircraft, including the parachute. Another story from the 1700s tells of a French locksmith named Besnier, who, with wings strapped to his arms and legs, jumped from a tall building and glided over neighboring houses.

The development of kites continued and they became the forerunners of free-flying airplanes. European inventors and scientists used them to carry out experiments in aerodynamic forces. Such experiments led to the first free-flying airplanes of Sir George Cayley in the 1790s. They demonstrated the principles of flight as they are understood today. In the 1850s Sir George's coachman was among the first people to fly in an actual airplane. The stage was now set for the development of controllable airplanes. That story is told through the paper airplanes that follow in this book.

Construction

When carefully made, the paper airplanes in this book are super flyers. They can be built using ordinary 20 or 24 lb bond copier paper measuring 8-1/2 in by 11 in (21.6cm by 27.9cm). Bond paper is lightweight, easy to cut and fold, and easy to fasten together. It is available in a variety of colors (black paper may have to be purchased from an art store). Since a paper airplane's lift and thrust are limited, every effort must be made to keep drag at a minimum. Every surface not parallel to the direction of travel (wings, nose, and canopy) adds drag, so the neater and more accurate your construction, the better the plane will fly. Clean and accurate cuts and crisp folds are a top priority.

Measuring and Cutting Use a sharp pencil to mark the measurements and draw firm, accurate lines. Cut out the pieces with a sharp pair of scissors or a craft knife and a steel-edged ruler. A knife makes a cleaner cut. When using a knife be sure to work on a proper cutting surface.

Folding Always lay the paper on a level surface for folding. Folding is easier along a score line (an indented line on the paper made with a hard pencil drawn along a ruler). There are only three kinds of folds used in making the airplanes in this book. They are mountain folds, valley folds, and sink folds. Where multiple layers are folded, run your fingers back and forth along the fold pressing hard to make a sharp crease.

Gluing A glue stick works well for paper airplanes. Follow the instructions for gluing. Cover the entire contacting surfaces that are to be joined. If there are multiple layers, apply glue to each of the sheets. Glue should be used sparingly, but use enough to hold the parts together. Where multiple layers are being joined you may need to hold the pieces for a few minutes until the glue sets.

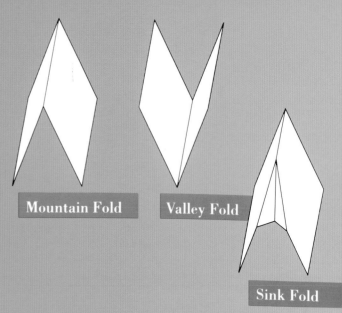

Mountain Fold **Valley Fold**

Sink Fold

A mountain fold and a valley fold are actually the same kind of fold. Both are made by folding a flat piece of paper and sharply creasing the fold line. The only difference is that one folds up (valley fold) and the other folds down (mountain fold). They are distinguished only for convenience in giving instructions.

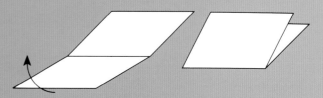

To make a sink fold, begin with paper that has been folded using a mountain (or valley) fold and measure as required across the folded corner. Then push in the corner along the measured lines, making a diagonal fold. Finish by creasing the folds sharply.

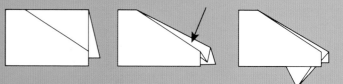

Trimming for Flight

Air is made up of small, solid, evenly spaced particles called molecules. Everything in the universe is made up of molecules, but air molecules are quite far apart compared to those that make up metal, wood, or paper, and they are easily separated when a body moves through them. The molecules are piled up in a thick layer from the ground, and this is called the atmosphere. It forms part of the space around us and the sky above us. This layer of air molecules (atmosphere) exerts pressure on everything in the world and it is this pressure that makes flight possible. The shape of the airplane affects the molecules as they move across the airplane's surfaces, increasing or decreasing air pressure, determining the flight characteristics of the plane.

No paper airplanes are perfectly straight. And they are easily bent. Shown right below is an example of trimming using the rudder. Airplane A flies straight because air flows smoothly along its surfaces. It needs no trim. Airplane B yaws to the left because the air on the left is deflected by the bent fuselage, increasing air pressure on that side. The rudder is used to compensate. Airplane C again flies straight because it has been trimmed so that the deflected air on the left is opposed by air being deflected by the rudder on the right. But airplane C does not fly as well as airplane A because it is creating much more drag.

Before making any trim adjustments to a paper airplane that you have just constructed, be sure you are releasing the plane correctly for flight. Always begin with a gentle straight-ahead release, keeping the wings level. Hold the plane between thumb and forefinger just behind the center of gravity. As your technique improves you can throw harder, adjusting the trim as needed. But remember, all planes do not fly at the same speed.

NOTE: Fly Safely. Some of the airplanes in this book have sharp points so never fly them toward another person. If you fly the airplanes outdoors they may go farther than you expect. Be sure they do not go into the street where you will have to retrieve them.

AIRPLANE CONTROL SURFACES

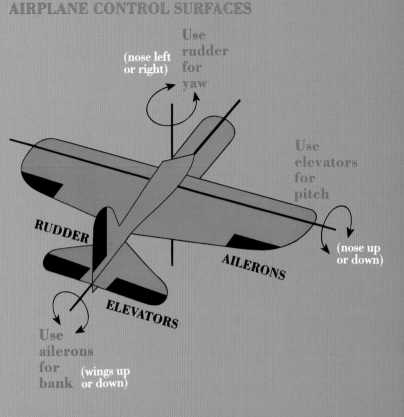

(nose left or right)

Use rudder for yaw

Use elevators for pitch

(nose up or down)

RUDDER

AILERONS

ELEVATORS

Use ailerons for bank

(wings up or down)

HOW TRIMMING WORKS

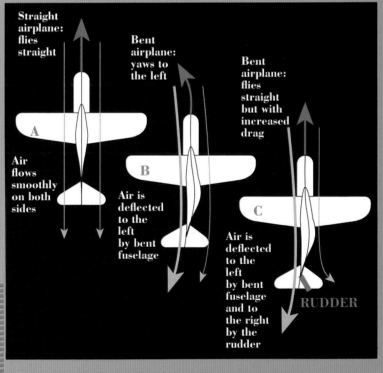

Straight airplane: flies straight

Bent airplane: yaws to the left

Bent airplane: flies straight but with increased drag

A

B

C

Air flows smoothly on both sides

Air is deflected to the left by bent fuselage

Air is deflected to the left by bent fuselage and to the right by the rudder

RUDDER

Aero Bat

HISTORICAL INFORMATION

The earliest aircraft designers looked to birds and bats for clues about airplane construction. They built them with thin wooden frames cross-braced with wires and covered in fabric. For control while in flight, the wing tips could be bent up or down as necessary by the pilot. But the airplanes were flimsy and difficult to fly. They often fluttered badly and some collapsed. Many crashed. Between the 1790s and the 1890s Sir George Cayley, Francis Wenham, Percy Pilcher, Lawrence Hargrave, Otto Lilienthal, and others, experimented with various bird-like airplane designs. This paper airplane is modeled on early bird-like planes.

Technical Information

Lift When a wing having a curved upper surface moves forward it slices the air into two layers – one above and one beneath the wing. Both air layers are made up of the same number of molecules, but those that move over the curved top of the wing have farther to go. So they must speed up and spread farther apart which causes them to exert less downward pressure. The molecules of air beneath the wing remain more closely spaced buoying up the airplane. Raising the leading edge of the wing slightly (the angle of attack), increases the difference in pressure above and below the wing, adding more buoyancy.

Gravity This force pulls everything in the world to the ground and opposes lift. Therefore an airplane's center of gravity (the point at which an object balances) must coincide with the lift created by the wings. If it doesn't the airplane is unstable. With the center of gravity too far back the nose will pitch up; too far forward and the nose will pitch down.

Making the Aero Bat

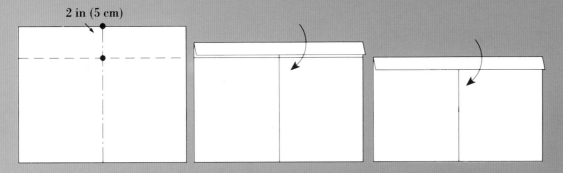

2 in (5 cm)

STEP 1 Lay the paper flat in a horizontal direction. Fold paper in half vertically, using the mountain fold. Unfold. Measure from upper edge and valley fold horizontally. Unfold. Then fold upper edge to meet horizontal crease. Refold original horizontal crease.

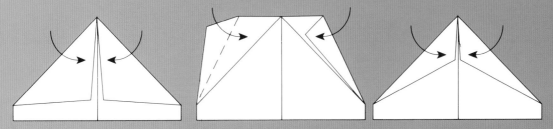

STEP 2 Valley fold upper corners to the vertical center crease. Unfold. Valley fold the upper corners to the diagonal creases. Then refold original diagonal creases.

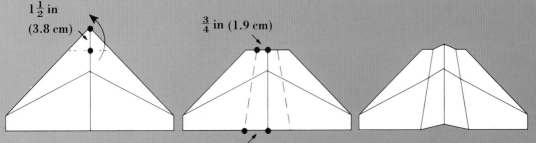

$1\frac{1}{2}$ in (3.8 cm)

$\frac{3}{4}$ in (1.9 cm)

$1\frac{1}{2}$ in (3.8 cm)

STEP 3 Measure from tip and mountain fold horizontally. On each side, measure and valley fold, as shown.

VIEW FROM BACK

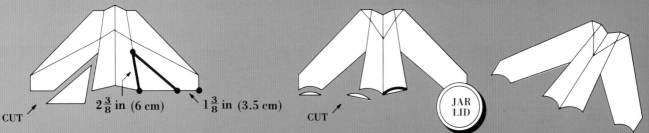

CUT

$2\frac{3}{8}$ in (6 cm) $1\frac{3}{8}$ in (3.5 cm)

CUT

JAR LID

STEP 4 On each side, measure and cut out triangles, as shown. Flip the airplane over. Then, using a small jar lid, trace scalloped edges and cut out, as shown. Adjust folds so that viewed from the back the plane forms an inverted W.

Sky Bird

Technical Information

Drag This is the force of resistance that air gives when objects move through it. Because of drag it is hard work to pedal your bike very fast. Drag also acts on an airplane in flight. It is responsible for slowing down a paper airplane.

Thrust This is the forward momentum of an airplane. After you launch a paper airplane the force of lift prevents gravity from pulling the plane straight down, but gravity is still at work. In a glider, gravity provides thrust. In flight the nose should point down slightly. In gliding flight, gravity will pull the plane along an invisible mass of air in a gentle downward movement, just as gravity pulls a sled down a hill. If the nose is pointed down too much the plane will dive and crash into the ground.

The four forces – lift, gravity, thrust, and drag – are always present acting together on an airplane in flight.

HISTORICAL INFORMATION

The first aircraft had no engines. They were gliders. Early airplane builders used high hills as launching points to test their constructions. The builders soon realized that in order for airplanes to fly successfully, having wings was not enough. Airplanes also needed horizontal and vertical surfaces for stability. Otto Lilienthal made many successful glider flights in the 1890s. This paper airplane is modeled on early glider aircraft.

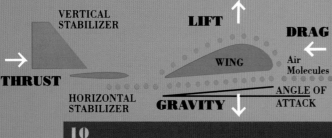

VERTICAL STABILIZER

LIFT

DRAG

THRUST

WING

Air Molecules

HORIZONTAL STABILIZER

GRAVITY

ANGLE OF ATTACK

Making the Sky Bird

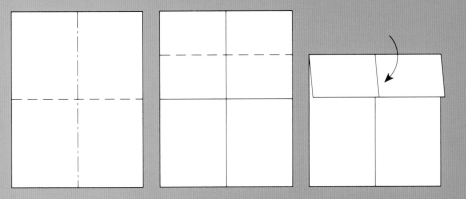

STEP 1   Lay paper flat in a vertical direction. Fold paper in half vertically using a mountain fold. Unfold. Valley fold the paper in half horizontally. Unfold. Then valley fold the top to meet the horizontal crease.

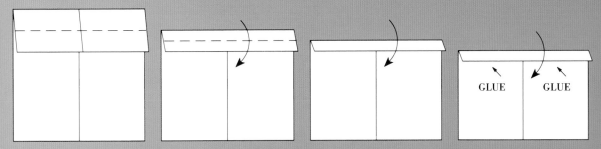

GLUE   GLUE

STEP 2   Valley fold the top again to meet the horizontal crease. Then valley fold top again, to meet the horizontal crease. Finally, applying glue to entire length, refold the original horizontal crease.

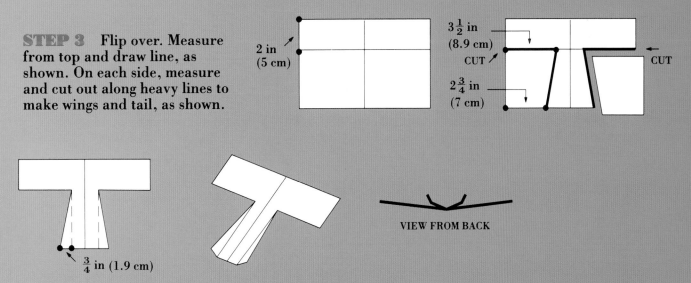

STEP 3   Flip over. Measure from top and draw line, as shown. On each side, measure and cut out along heavy lines to make wings and tail, as shown.

2 in (5 cm)

3 $\frac{1}{2}$ in (8.9 cm)   CUT

2 $\frac{3}{4}$ in (7 cm)

CUT

$\frac{3}{4}$ in (1.9 cm)

VIEW FROM BACK

STEP 4   On each side of tail, measure and valley fold. Adjust dihedral (upward slanting of wings and tail), as shown.

STEP 5 Cut the two pieces left over from step 3 into rectangles, as shown.

STEP 6 To make the fuselage (body), valley fold piece A in half horizontally. Glue halves together.

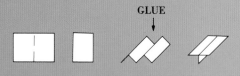

GLUE

STEP 7 Valley fold this piece in half vertically. Then fold each vertical edge back to meet center crease. Glue center section. This is the fuselage.

STEP 8 To make nose ballast, valley fold piece B in half horizontally. Glue halves together. Valley fold in half vertically. Glue halves together. Then valley fold in half horizontally. Glue halves together. Finally, valley fold in half vertically.

GLUE
IN PLACE

STEP 9 Glue this piece to the bottom of the center section of the fuselage, aligning at one of the ends. This end becomes the front.

1 in (2.5 cm)

STEP 10 Measure from front of fuselage and mark the point, as shown.

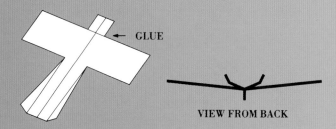

GLUE

VIEW FROM BACK

STEP 11 Glue wings and tail to the fuselage with the leading edge (front of the wings) at the measured point. Make sure pieces are centered. Adjust dihedral (upward slanting of wings and tail) again.

12

Plain Plane

HISTORICAL INFORMATION

Achieving stability in flight was a major concern for early airplane designers, and remains so today. In the early days many different airplane shapes were tried. The most practical arrangement of parts had wings near the middle attached to a fuselage (body) with a tail at the back that had both horizontal and vertical surfaces. The fuselage also had room for the pilot. This arrangement has become the conventional and most often used aircraft design. Movable surfaces were added to the trailing (back) edges of wings and stabilizers: ailerons on the wing tips controlled roll (rotation along the length of an airplane), elevators on the horizontal tail controled pitch (nose up or down), and a rudder on the vertical tail controled yaw (nose left or right). This paper airplane is modeled on the conventional airplane.

Technical Information

If an airplane is to be stable in flight, it is important to get the center of gravity in the correct spot. (The planes in this book are designed with the correct center of gravity location, but if more ballast is needed, add it to the nose by using a small piece of paper, a dab of plasticine, some clear tape, or a small pin.) For best construction results use the 20 or 24 lb bond copier paper recommended, measure accurately, and make crisp folds. Use glue sparingly, but use enough to hold the parts together.

While an airplane is in flight the four forces (lift, gravity, thrust, and drag) must be in balance. Then the airplane is in trim for straight and level flight. Paper airplanes need frequent small adjustments to the control surfaces in order to fly well. You may need to make different trim adjustments for indoor flight than for outdoor flight in lively air. Always make small corrections. Remember, a small adjustment has a big effect.

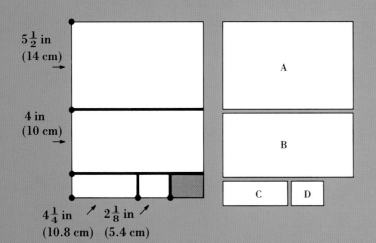

5 ½ in
(14 cm)

4 in
(10 cm)

A

B

C   D

4 ¼ in   2 ⅛ in
(10.8 cm) (5.4 cm)

STEP 1 Measure and cut the various pieces from a sheet of bond paper, as shown.

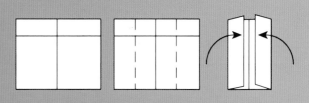

STEP 2 Lay piece A flat in a vertical direction. To make the fuselage, fold in half vertically using a valley fold. Unfold. Valley fold in half horizontally. Unfold. Then valley fold the top to meet the horizontal crease.

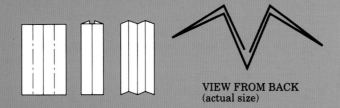

STEP 3 Valley fold the top again to meet the horizontal crease. Refold the original crease.

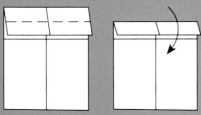

STEP 4 Valley fold each side so that outer edges meet center crease, as shown.

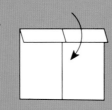

VIEW FROM BACK
(actual size)

STEP 5 Fold each side again using a mountain fold, so that outer edges meet center crease at back. Then adjust folds so the paper looks like an upside-down W, as shown.

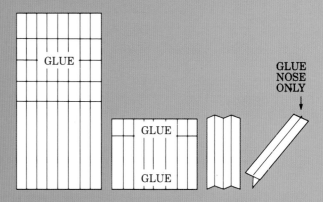

GLUE

GLUE

GLUE

GLUE
NOSE
ONLY

STEP 6 Unfold fuselage (piece A) completely. Refold applying glue to contacting surfaces, as shown. Make sure fuselage is straight.

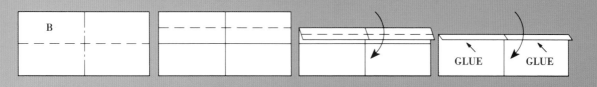

STEP 7 Use piece B to make the wings. Lay paper flat horizontally. Fold in half vertically, using a mountain fold. Unfold. Fold in half horizontally, using a valley fold. Unfold. Then valley fold so that top edge meets center crease. Fold again so that top edge meets center crease. Applying glue to entire length, refold original horizontal center crease. The folded over part is the bottom of the leading edge (front) of the wings.

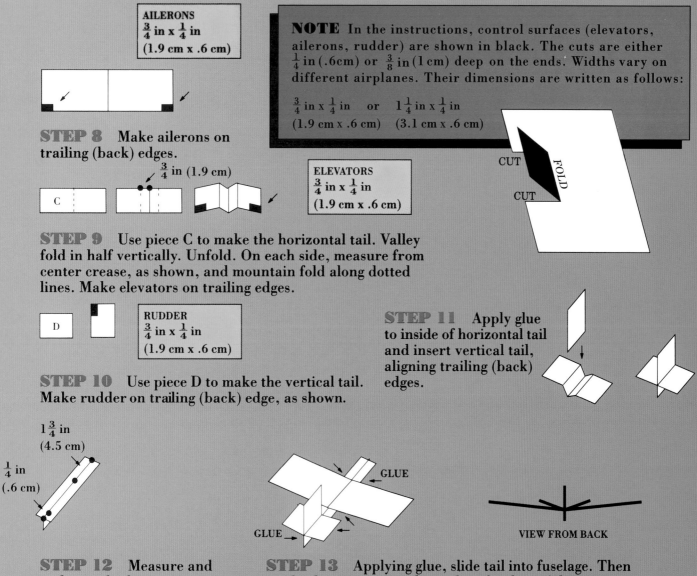

> **AILERONS**
> $\frac{3}{4}$ in x $\frac{1}{4}$ in
> (1.9 cm x .6 cm)

NOTE In the instructions, control surfaces (elevators, ailerons, rudder) are shown in black. The cuts are either $\frac{1}{4}$ in (.6cm) or $\frac{3}{8}$ in (1 cm) deep on the ends. Widths vary on different airplanes. Their dimensions are written as follows:

$\frac{3}{4}$ in x $\frac{1}{4}$ in   or $1\frac{1}{4}$ in x $\frac{1}{4}$ in
(1.9 cm x .6 cm)   (3.1 cm x .6 cm)

CUT
FOLD
CUT

STEP 8 Make ailerons on trailing (back) edges.

$\frac{3}{4}$ in (1.9 cm)

C

> **ELEVATORS**
> $\frac{3}{4}$ in x $\frac{1}{4}$ in
> (1.9 cm x .6 cm)

STEP 9 Use piece C to make the horizontal tail. Valley fold in half vertically. Unfold. On each side, measure from center crease, as shown, and mountain fold along dotted lines. Make elevators on trailing edges.

D

> **RUDDER**
> $\frac{3}{4}$ in x $\frac{1}{4}$ in
> (1.9 cm x .6 cm)

STEP 11 Apply glue to inside of horizontal tail and insert vertical tail, aligning trailing (back) edges.

STEP 10 Use piece D to make the vertical tail. Make rudder on trailing (back) edge, as shown.

$1\frac{3}{4}$ in
(4.5 cm)

$\frac{1}{4}$ in
(.6 cm)

GLUE

GLUE

VIEW FROM BACK

STEP 12 Measure and make marks for positioning tail and wings.

STEP 13 Applying glue, slide tail into fuselage. Then apply glue to wings and attach to fuselage. Adjust dihedral (upward slanting of wings and tail).

Biplane

HISTORICAL INFORMATION

One way to improve lift without making large wings was by having two sets of them, one above the other (biplanes). The box-like construction of these airplanes made it easy to cross-brace the lightweight wooden frames with wire for strength. In 1903 Orville and Wilbur Wright put an engine into a biplane and became the first to attain sustained powered flight. Biplanes were used for most of the air battles of World War I, which began in 1914. Fighter biplanes were highly maneuverable although difficult to handle. Some examples are the Spad 7, Sopwith Camel, and Fokker 7. Biplanes are now used where small, durable, and maneuverable airplanes are required. Crop spraying is a good example. This paper airplane is modeled on early biplanes.

Technical Information

Biplanes have stubby noses and short wings and tails, making them sensitive to pitch and roll because the distances from the center of gravity to the control surfaces are small. The planes require careful trimming

If the airplane zooms nose down to the ground, bend the elevators up slightly to raise the nose in flight.

This may cause the nose of the plane to pitch up sharply. As a result the air no longer flows smoothly over the wing surfaces but separates into eddies and the wings stall. To solve this problem bend the elevators up less.

If the elevators are not bent at all and the nose still rises, don't bend the elevators down to correct the problem (a plane should never fly this way). Rather add a bit of extra ballast to the nose.

If the plane veers to left or right, bend the aileron up slightly on the wing that rises and down slightly on the wing that falls. Also bend the rudder on the vertical tail slightly, opposite to the direction of the turn.

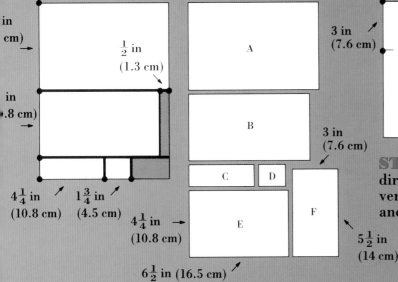

in
cm)

$\frac{1}{2}$ in
(1.3 cm)

in
.8 cm)

A

B

C   D

E

F

$4\frac{1}{4}$ in
(10.8 cm)

$1\frac{3}{4}$ in
(4.5 cm)

$4\frac{1}{4}$ in
(10.8 cm)

3 in
(7.6 cm)

$5\frac{1}{2}$ in
(14 cm)

$6\frac{1}{2}$ in (16.5 cm)

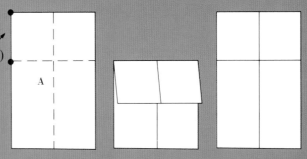

3 in
(7.6 cm)

A

STEP 2   Lay piece A flat in a vertical direction. To make the fuselage, fold in half vertically using a valley fold. Unfold. Measure and valley fold horizontally, as shown. Unfold.

STEP 1   Measure and cut the various pieces from a sheet of bond paper, as shown. Two additional pieces E and F are needed, as shown.

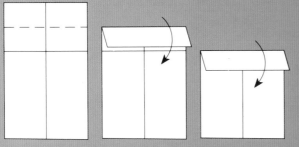

STEP 3   Valley fold the top to meet the horizontal crease. Then refold the original horizontal crease.

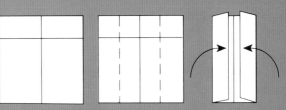

STEP 4   Valley fold each side so that outer edges meet center crease, as shown.

VIEW FROM BACK
(actual size)

STEP 5   Fold each side again using a mountain fold, so that outer edges meet center crease at back. Then adjust folds so that paper looks like an upside-down W, as shown.

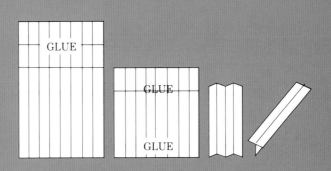

GLUE

GLUE

GLUE

STEP 6   Unfold fuselage completely. Refold applying glue to all contacting surfaces, as shown. Make sure fuselage is straight. Do not glue nose yet.

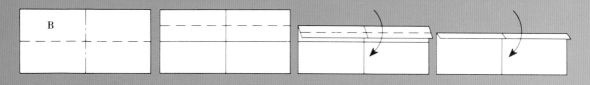

STEP 7 Lay piece B in a horizontal position to make the lower wings. Fold in half vertically, using a mountain fold. Unfold. Fold in half horizontally, using a valley fold. Unfold. Then valley fold so that top edge meets center crease. Fold again so that top edge meets center crease. Refold original horizontal center crease.

$1\frac{5}{8}$ in
(4.1 cm)

STEP 8 Unfold completely. On each side, measure and cut diagonally, as shown. Refold. Apply glue before refolding original horizontal center crease only. The folded over part is the bottom of the leading edge (front) of the wings.

$\frac{1}{2}$ in
(1.3 cm)

$\frac{3}{4}$ in
(1.9 cm)

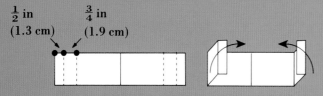

STEP 9 On each side, measure and valley fold, as shown.

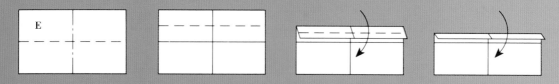

STEP 10 Lay piece E horizontally to make the upper wings. Fold in half vertically, using a mountain fold. Unfold. Fold in half horizontally, using a valley fold. Unfold. Then valley fold so that top edge meets center crease. Fold again so that top edge meets center crease. Refold original horizontal center crease.

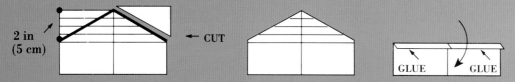

2 in
(5 cm)

STEP 11 Unfold completely. On each side, measure and cut diagonally, as shown. Refold. Apply glue before refolding original horizontal center crease only. The folded over part is the bottom of the leading edge (front) of the wings.

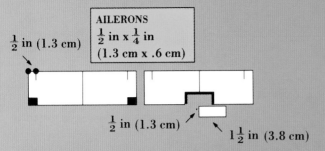

AILERONS
$\frac{1}{2}$ in x $\frac{1}{4}$ in
(1.3 cm x .6 cm)

$\frac{1}{2}$ in (1.3 cm)

$\frac{1}{2}$ in (1.3 cm)

$1\frac{1}{2}$ in (3.8 cm)

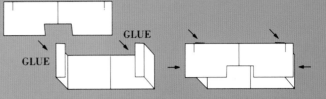

GLUE

GLUE

STEP 12 On each side of upper wings, measure from each wing tip and mark attachment points for lower wings, as shown. Cut out center piece on trailing edge, as shown. Make ailerons in locations indicated.

STEP 13 Applying glue, fasten upper and lower wings together, as shown. Make sure both leading edges face the same direction.

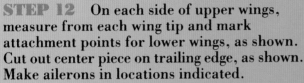

$\frac{3}{4}$ in (1.9 cm)

$\frac{5}{8}$ in (1.6 cm)

ELEVATORS
$1\frac{1}{4}$ in x $\frac{1}{4}$ in
(3.1 cm x .6 cm)

STEP 14 Use piece C to make the horizontal tail. Valley fold in half vertically. Unfold. On each side, measure from outer edges, as shown, and cut along heavy lines. Then, on each side, measure from center crease and mountain fold, as shown. Make elevators.

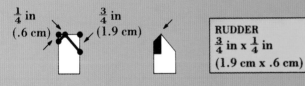

$\frac{1}{4}$ in (.6 cm)

$\frac{3}{4}$ in (1.9 cm)

RUDDER
$\frac{3}{4}$ in x $\frac{1}{4}$ in
(1.9 cm x .6 cm)

STEP 15 Measure and cut leading edge along heavy lines, as shown. On trailing edge, make rudder.

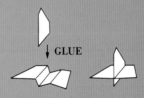

GLUE

STEP 16 Apply glue to inside of horizontal tail and insert vertical tail, aligning trailing (back) edges.

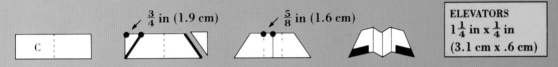

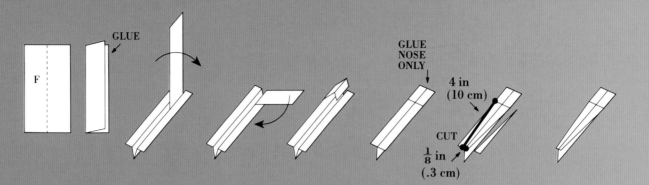

STEP 17   Use piece F to make the nose cowl (ballast). Valley fold piece in half vertically. Glue halves together. Applying glue to one side, insert F into nose and wrap entirely around fuselage, as shown. Then glue fuselage together at nose only.

STEP 18   On each side, measure and cut fuselage back along heavy lines, as shown.

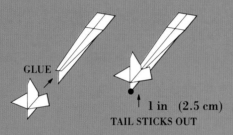

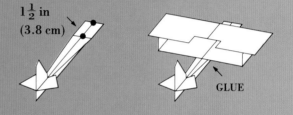

STEP 19   Applying glue, slide the tail into the back of the fuselelage.

STEP 20   Measure from front of fuselage and mark front of wing position. Glue wings in place, as shown.

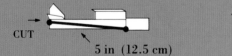

VIEW FROM BACK

STEP 21   Measure and cut back of fuselage, as shown. Adjust dihedral (upward slanting of wings and tail) to finish airplane.

Aero Stunt

STUNTPLANE

HISTORICAL INFORMATION

Ever since the earliest days of flight, flying events attracted great crowds of spectators. After World War I, many pilots performed aerial maneuvers learned in combat as stunts for entertainment. Sometimes people walked on the wings, or even jumped from one plane to another, while the airplanes were in flight. Such events (called barnstorming) thrilled spectators, and even today, air shows where aerobatics are performed, draw huge crowds. As planes improved, air racing became popular. Speeds exceeded 200 mph. This paper airplane is designed specifically to do stunts. It will not fly straight and level.

Technical Information

Loops When an airplane flies a loop it must maintain its speed throughout the entire maneuver. Making a round loop depends on centrifugal force. This force pushes the plane outwards, much like swinging a ball on a string. Only there is no string to hold it. Instead, the plane's wings create a centripedal force that keeps it from flying off and distorting the loop.

Rolls When the ailerons are used, one bends upwards and the other one bends down. This causes the airplane to bank in the direction of the upward bent aileron. A powered airplane can roll completely, over and over, flying along in corkscrew fashion.

Hammerheads In this maneuver the airplane is flown straight up, but before it stalls the plane is turned so that it points straight down, swooping smoothly out of the dive.

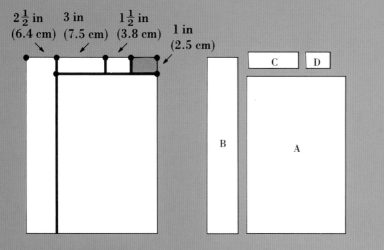

2½ in (6.4 cm) 3 in (7.5 cm) 1½ in (3.8 cm) 1 in (2.5 cm)

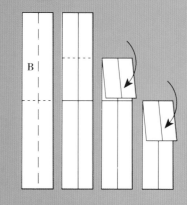

STEP 1 Measure and cut four pieces from a sheet of bond paper, as shown.

STEP 2 Lay piece B vertically to make the fuselage. Valley fold in half vertically. Unfold. Valley fold in half horizontally. Unfold. Valley fold so that upper edge meets the horizontal crease. Then refold the original horizontal crease.

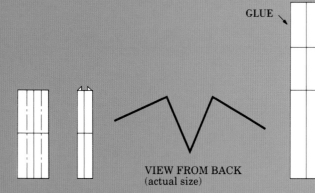

VIEW FROM BACK
(actual size)

GLUE

GLUE

STEP 3 Fold each side using a mountain fold so that outer edges meet center crease at back. Then adjust folds so that paper looks like an upside-down W, as shown.

STEP 4 Unfold fuselage completely. Refold applying glue to all contacting surfaces, as shown. Make sure fuselage is straight.

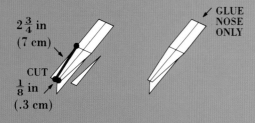

2¾ in (7 cm)

CUT

⅛ in (.3 cm)

GLUE NOSE ONLY

STEP 5 On each side, measure and cut fuselage back along heavy lines, as shown. Then glue nose only.

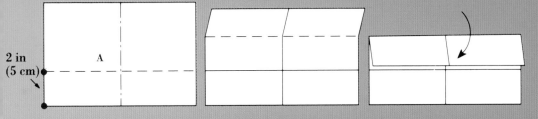

STEP 6 Lay piece A horizontally to make the wings. Fold in half vertically, using a mountain fold. Unfold. Measure from the bottom and fold horizontally, using a valley fold. Unfold. Then valley fold so that top edge meets horizontal crease.

2 in (5 cm)

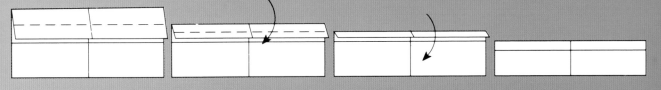

STEP 7 Valley fold so that top edge meets horizontal crease. Again valley fold so that top edge meets horizontal crease. Then refold original horizontal crease.

NOTE: Control surfaces for this plane are different from all the others.

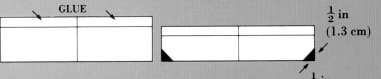

GLUE

½ in (1.3 cm)

½ in (1.3 cm)

STEP 8 Unfold the last fold only and apply glue to entire length. Refold. Make ailerons by folding diagonally, as shown.

½ in (1.3 cm)   ½ in (1.3 cm)

C

STEP 9 Use piece C to make the horizontal tail. Valley fold in half vertically. Unfold. On each side, measure from center crease and mountain fold, as shown. Make elevators by folding diagonally, as shown.

½ in (1.3 cm)

½ in (1.3 cm)

D

GLUE

STEP 10 Use piece D for the vertical tail. Measure and cut diagonally along heavy line, as shown. Then apply glue to inside of horizontal tail and insert vertical tail, aligning trailing (back) edges.

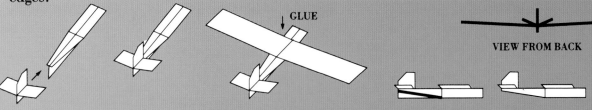

GLUE

VIEW FROM BACK

STEP 11 Applying glue, slide the tail into the back of fuselage, aligning trailing edges.

STEP 12 Applying glue, attach wings so that trailing edges align with seam on the fuselage.

STEP 13 Cut fuselage diagonally from the seam to the back, as shown by heavy line. Adjust dihedral (upward slanting of wings and tail), as shown.

23

Gee Bee Racer

Technical Information

The Gee Bee model R is mostly a flying engine. Its big radial engine produces over 500 horsepower. Drag is the enemy of the racer. To go fast, even with a powerful engine, drag must be kept at a minimum. When this plane was being designed, different shapes were tested in a wind tunnel to find a shape that had the least amount of drag. A fat and stubby "teardrop" shape was found to be ideal. But such a stubby shape makes for a tempermental plane to fly. All airplanes that are stubby with short wings and tails are sensitive to pitch and roll because the distances from the center of gravity to the control surfaces are short. This paper model, however, is a remarkably good flyer.

HISTORICAL INFORMATION

From the very beginning of powered flight, it became apparent that airplanes and speed belonged together. Air races were established so that builders could compete with one another. Three popular races were the Thompson Race, the Bendix Race, and the Shell Speed Dash. In 1932 the Granville brothers built the Gee Bee model R racer to compete in all three races. Two R models were built. That year they won the Thompson and set a new Speed Dash record of almost 300 mph. It takes great skill to fly at high speed near the ground in a tempermental airplane such as a racer. Both planes eventually crashed, and two pilots lost their lives. Today another Gee Bee, just like the originals, has been built. It is a popular attraction at many air shows.

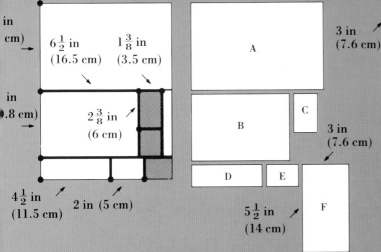

6 $\frac{1}{2}$ in (16.5 cm)
1 $\frac{3}{8}$ in (3.5 cm)
2 $\frac{3}{8}$ in (6 cm)
in cm)
in 0.8 cm)
4 $\frac{1}{2}$ in (11.5 cm)
2 in (5 cm)

A
B
C
D
E
F
5 $\frac{1}{2}$ in (14 cm)
3 in (7.6 cm)

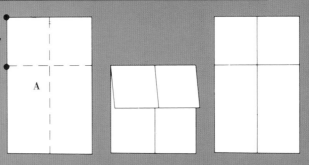

3 in (7.6 cm)
A

STEP 2 Lay piece A flat in a vertical direction. Fold in half vertically using a valley fold, to make the fuselage. Unfold. Measure and valley fold horizontally, as shown. Unfold.

STEP 1 Measure and cut the various pieces from a sheet of bond paper, as shown. One additional piece F is needed, as shown.

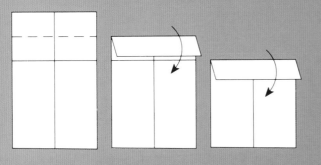

STEP 3 Valley fold the top to meet the horizontal crease. Then refold the original horizontal crease.

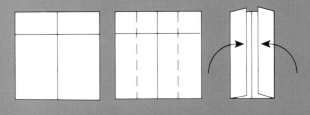

STEP 4 Valley fold each side so that outer edges meet center crease, as shown.

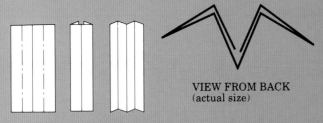

VIEW FROM BACK (actual size)

STEP 5 Fold each side again using a mountain fold, so that outer edges meet center crease at back. Then adjust folds so that paper looks like an upside-down W, as shown.

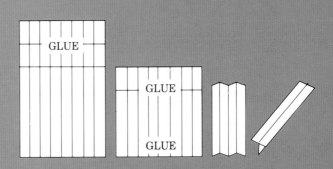

GLUE
GLUE
GLUE

STEP 6 Unfold fuselage completely. Refold applying glue to all contacting surfaces, as shown. Make sure fuselage is straight. Do not glue nose yet.

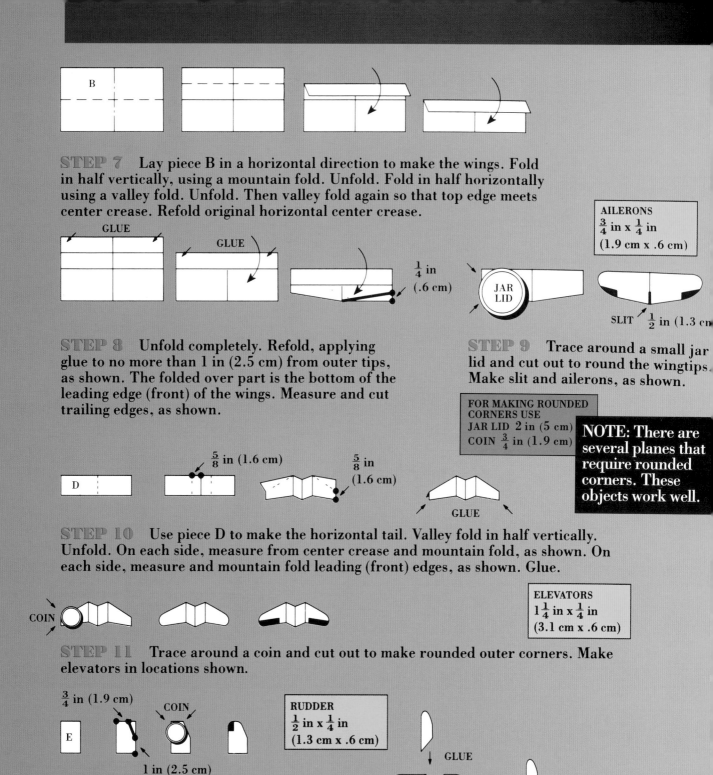

STEP 7 Lay piece B in a horizontal direction to make the wings. Fold in half vertically, using a mountain fold. Unfold. Fold in half horizontally using a valley fold. Unfold. Then valley fold again so that top edge meets center crease. Refold original horizontal center crease.

GLUE

GLUE

$\frac{1}{4}$ in (.6 cm)

AILERONS
$\frac{3}{4}$ in x $\frac{1}{4}$ in
(1.9 cm x .6 cm)

JAR LID

SLIT $\frac{1}{2}$ in (1.3 cm

STEP 8 Unfold completely. Refold, applying glue to no more than 1 in (2.5 cm) from outer tips, as shown. The folded over part is the bottom of the leading edge (front) of the wings. Measure and cut trailing edges, as shown.

STEP 9 Trace around a small jar lid and cut out to round the wingtips. Make slit and ailerons, as shown.

FOR MAKING ROUNDED CORNERS USE
JAR LID 2 in (5 cm)
COIN $\frac{3}{4}$ in (1.9 cm)

NOTE: There are several planes that require rounded corners. These objects work well.

D

$\frac{5}{8}$ in (1.6 cm)

$\frac{5}{8}$ in (1.6 cm)

GLUE

STEP 10 Use piece D to make the horizontal tail. Valley fold in half vertically. Unfold. On each side, measure from center crease and mountain fold, as shown. On each side, measure and mountain fold leading (front) edges, as shown. Glue.

ELEVATORS
$1\frac{1}{4}$ in x $\frac{1}{4}$ in
(3.1 cm x .6 cm)

COIN

STEP 11 Trace around a coin and cut out to make rounded outer corners. Make elevators in locations shown.

$\frac{3}{4}$ in (1.9 cm)

COIN

E

RUDDER
$\frac{1}{2}$ in x $\frac{1}{4}$ in
(1.3 cm x .6 cm)

1 in (2.5 cm)

GLUE

STEP 12 Use piece E to make the vertical tail. Measure and cut leading (front) edge as shown by heavy line. Trace around a coin and cut out to round corners. On trailing edge, make rudder.

STEP 13 Apply glue to inside of horizontal tail and insert vertical tail, aligning trailing (back) edges.

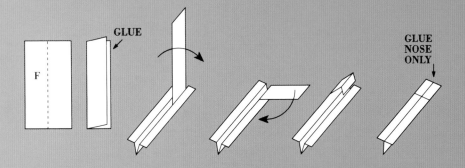

STEP 14 Use piece F to make the nose cowl (ballast). Valley fold piece in half vertically. Glue halves together. Applying glue to one side, insert F into nose and wrap entirely around fuselage, as shown. Then glue fuselage together at nose only.

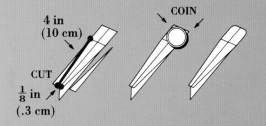

STEP 15 On each side, measure and cut fuselage back along heavy lines, as shown. Trace around a coin and cut out to round the nose.

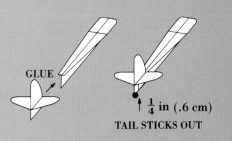

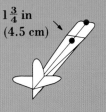

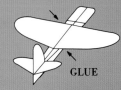

STEP 16 Applying glue, slide the tail into the back of the fuselage.

STEP 17 Measure from front of fuselage and mark front of wing position. Glue wings in place, as shown.

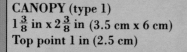

CANOPY (type 1)
$1\frac{3}{8}$ in x $2\frac{3}{8}$ in (3.5 cm x 6 cm)
Top point 1 in (2.5 cm)

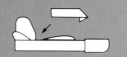

SLIT 1 in (2.5 cm)

STEP 18 Make the canopy, using piece C (see below). Make a slit at the center back, as shown.

STEP 19 Apply glue to the inside back and front tab of the canopy. Insert tab into the fuselage, sliding the vertical tail into the slit.

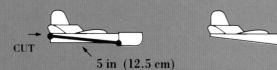

CUT

5 in (12.5 cm)

VIEW FROM BACK

STEP 20 Measure and cut back of fuselage, as shown. Adjust dihedral (upward slanting of wings and tail) to finish airplane.

NOTE This is the first airplane design in this book to have a canopy. The canopy adds realism as well as ballast. There are two main types, as shown below. Dimensions are given with each airplane design.

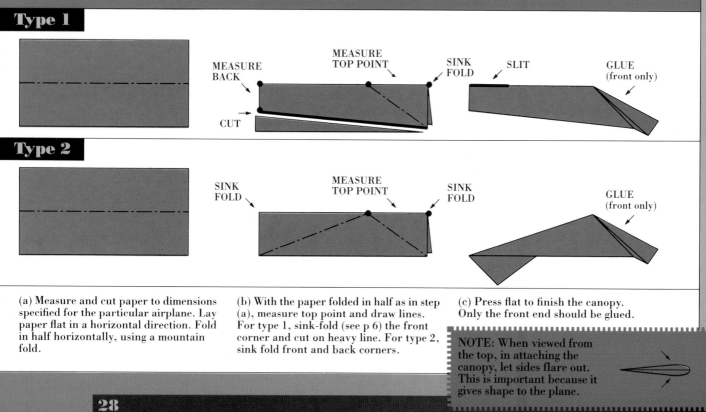

Type 1

MEASURE
BACK

MEASURE
TOP POINT

SINK
FOLD

SLIT

GLUE
(front only)

CUT

Type 2

SINK
FOLD

MEASURE
TOP POINT

SINK
FOLD

GLUE
(front only)

(a) Measure and cut paper to dimensions specified for the particular airplane. Lay paper flat in a horizontal direction. Fold in half horizontally, using a mountain fold.

(b) With the paper folded in half as in step (a), measure top point and draw lines. For type 1, sink-fold (see p 6) the front corner and cut on heavy line. For type 2, sink fold front and back corners.

(c) Press flat to finish the canopy. Only the front end should be glued.

NOTE: When viewed from the top, in attaching the canopy, let sides flare out. This is important because it gives shape to the plane.

P47 Thunderbolt

HISTORICAL INFORMATION

With the outbreak of another world war in 1939, there was again a demand for maneuverable fighter planes. Streamlined airframes capable of great speed were designed. More powerful engines were made, pushing speeds past 400 mph. Some popular examples of fighters are the Republic P47, North American P51, Supermarine Spitfire, Messerschmitt ME109, and the Mitsubishi "Zero". After the war ended in 1945 some of these warplanes became sport planes, and these inspired the building of aircraft using aerodynamic and technical information gained from fighter design. This paper airplane is modeled on the fighters of World War II and present-day sport planes.

Technical Information

Speed and Drag: From the very beginning of powered flight it was realized that speed and flight belonged together. The unobstructed freedom that flying offered, combined with speed, made it easy and fast to get from place to place. The biplanes of World War I, with engines about as powerful as those found in a small car, could exceed 100 mph. The fighters of World War II, with much more powerful engines, could exceed 400 mph. With such an increase in speed, drag also increased and airplane builders had to find ways to reduce it as much as possible. One way was by rounding corners and removing things that stuck out into the airflow (streamlining) and hiding them underneath a smooth skin.

In slow flight (as in landing) airplanes that can fly fast need a method of increasing the lift of their high-speed wings. They have secondary control surfaces, called flaps, that bend down on the trailing edges of the wings near the fuselage. Flaps are used not only when landing but also for takeoff or whenever extra lift is needed.

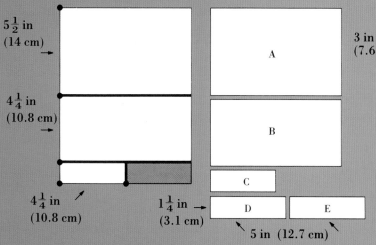

$5\frac{1}{2}$ in (14 cm)

$4\frac{1}{4}$ in (10.8 cm)

$4\frac{1}{4}$ in (10.8 cm)

$1\frac{1}{4}$ in (3.1 cm)

5 in (12.7 cm)

A

B

C

D   E

STEP 1   Measure and cut the various pieces from a sheet of bond paper, as shown. Two additional pieces D and E are needed, as shown.

3 in (7.6 cm)

A

STEP 2   Lay piece A flat in a vertical direction to make the fuselage. Fold in half vertically using a valley fold. Unfold. Measure and valley fold horizontally, as shown. Unfold

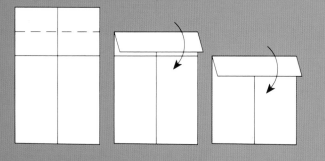

STEP 3   Valley fold the top to meet the horizontal crease. Then refold the original horizontal crease.

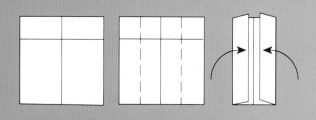

STEP 4   Valley fold each side so that outer edges meet center crease, as shown.

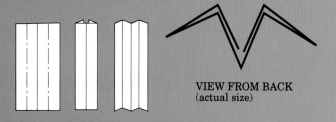

VIEW FROM BACK (actual size)

STEP 5   Fold each side again using a mountain fold, so that outer edges meet center crease at back. Then adjust folds so that paper looks like an upside-down W, as shown.

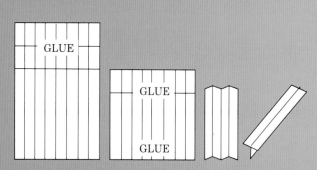

GLUE

GLUE

GLUE

STEP 6   Unfold fuselage completely. Refold applying glue to all contacting surfaces, as shown. Make sure fuselage is straight. Do not glue nose yet.

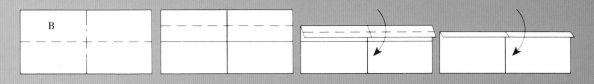

STEP 7 Lay piece B horizontally to make the wings. Fold in half vertically, using a mountain fold. Unfold. Fold in half horizontally, using a valley fold. Unfold. Then valley fold so that top edge meets center crease. Fold again so that top edge meets center crease. Refold original horizontal center crease.

$\frac{5}{8}$ in (4.1 cm)

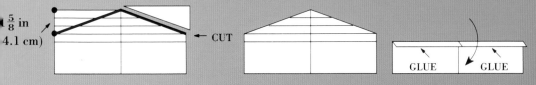

← CUT

GLUE   GLUE

STEP 8 Unfold completely. On each side, measure and cut diagonally, as shown. Refold. Apply glue before refolding original horizontal center crease only. The folded over part is the bottom of the leading edge (front) of the wings.

$1\frac{5}{8}$ in (4.1 cm)

← CUT

JAR LID   COIN

STEP 9 Measure and cut trailing edge (back) of wings, as shown. Trace around a coin to make rounded corners at the leading edges and a small jar lid for the trailing edge, and cut out (see p 26). Make ailerons, as shown.

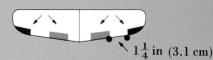

$1\frac{1}{4}$ in (3.1 cm)

AILERONS
1 in x $\frac{1}{4}$ in
(2.5 cm x .6 cm)

FLAPS
$1\frac{1}{4}$ in x $\frac{1}{4}$ in
(3.1 cm x .6 cm)

NOTE: In the instructions, secondary control surfaces (flaps) are shown in red.

STEP 10 On trailing edges, make ailerons. Then make secondary control surfaces (flaps), in locations shown.

$\frac{5}{8}$ in (1.6 cm)

$\frac{3}{4}$ in (1.9 cm)

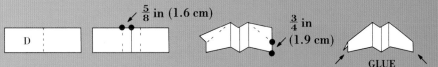

GLUE

STEP 11 Use piece D to make the horizontal tail. Valley fold in half vertically. Unfold. On each side, measure from center crease, as shown, and mountain fold. On each side, measure and mountain fold leading (front) edges, as shown. Glue.

ELEVATORS
$1\frac{1}{2}$ in x $\frac{1}{4}$ in
(3.8 cm x .6 cm)

COIN

STEP 12 Trace around a coin and cut out to make all the corners rounded (see p 26). Make elevators, as shown.

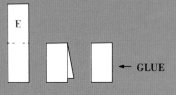

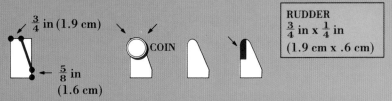

RUDDER
$\frac{3}{4}$ in x $\frac{1}{4}$ in
(1.9 cm x .6 cm)

$\frac{3}{4}$ in (1.9 cm)

$\frac{5}{8}$ in
(1.6 cm)

COIN

STEP 13   Use piece E to make the vertical tail. Mountain fold in half horizontally, glue halves together.

STEP 14   Measure and cut leading edge along heavy line, as shown. Trace around a coin and cut out to round corners (see p 26). On trailing (back) edge, make rudder.

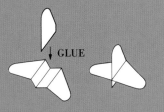

GLUE

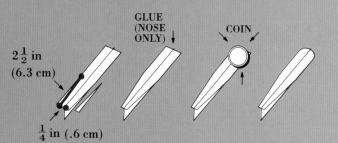

GLUE (NOSE ONLY)

COIN

$2\frac{1}{2}$ in (6.3 cm)

$\frac{1}{4}$ in (.6 cm)

STEP 15   Apply glue to inside of horizontal tail and insert vertical tail, aligning trailing (back) edges.

STEP 16   On each side, measure and cut fuselage back, as shown. Then glue nose only. To round corners, trace around a coin and cut out all corners of the nose (see p 26).

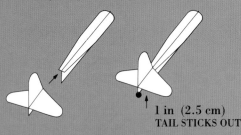

1 in (2.5 cm)
TAIL STICKS OUT

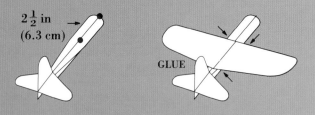

$2\frac{1}{2}$ in (6.3 cm)

GLUE

STEP 17   Applying glue, slide the tail into back of fuselage.

STEP 18   Measure from front of fuselage and glue wings in place, as shown.

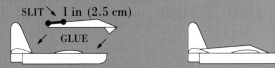

SLIT   1 in (2.5 cm)

GLUE

CANOPY (type 1)
$1\frac{1}{4}$ in x $4\frac{1}{4}$ in (3.1 cm x 10.8 cm)
Top point 1 in (2.5 cm)
Back $\frac{3}{8}$ in (1 cm)

STEP 19   Make a type 1 canopy, using piece C (See p 28). Cut slit in back of canopy. Apply glue to inside back of canopy and the front tab. Slip back over vertical tail and front tab into fuselage, as shown.

CUT

4 in (10 cm)

VIEW FROM BACK

STEP 20   Measure and cut back of fuselage along heavy line, as shown. Adjust dihedral (upward slanting of wings and tail), as shown.

DH108 Swallow

HISTORICAL INFORMATION

Beyond a certain speed conventional airplanes become less controllable and propellers lose their efficiency. When aircraft approach the speed of sound (about 760 mph) their control becomes unpredictable due to air resistance. For high speed flight a new shape of airplane was needed. For propulsion, designers turned to rockets and jets, which don't need propellers. In the quest for greater speed, Messerschmitt experimented with a rocket propelled airplane during the war, the ME163. After the war, deHavilland used the information gained to build the similar, but jet engined, experimental DH108 Swallow. It had wings that swept back and no horizontal stabilizers. In 1946 it flew over 600 mph. This paper airplane is modeled on the deHavilland Swallow.

Technical Information

Sweepback: Every increase in speed increases drag. Below a speed of about 250 mph air molecules easily move around a well streamlined airplane's surfaces. As speed is increased, however, the molecules cannot move out of the way quickly enough and their resistance piles them up into a pressure ridge ahead of the wings, something like a snowplow pushing snow. This build-up of pressure (drag) makes it difficult to fly the airplane, and at the speed of sound it can become dangerous. Sweeping the wings back away from the fuselage and making them broader delayed the pressure build-up until a greater speed was reached. This resulted in wings that maintain their efficiency, safely allowing planes to fly faster.

The experimental Swallow was built to test high speed flight. But even with swept-back wings, when this plane reached the speed of sound, the pressure build-up was great enough to break the airplane, and it crashed.

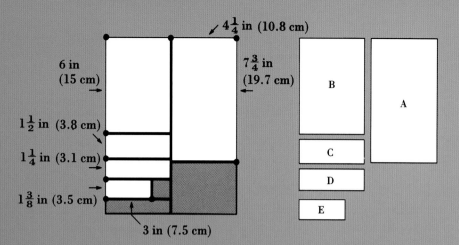

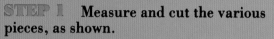

4¼ in (10.8 cm)

6 in (15 cm)

7¾ in (19.7 cm)

1½ in (3.8 cm)

1¼ in (3.1 cm)

1⅜ in (3.5 cm)

3 in (7.5 cm)

B

A

C

D

E

STEP 1   Measure and cut the various pieces, as shown.

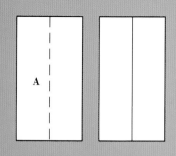

A

STEP 2   Lay piece A flat in a vertical direction. To make the fuselage, fold in half vertically using a valley fold. Unfold.

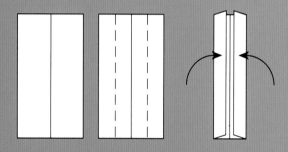

STEP 3   Valley fold each outer edge to meet center crease, as shown.

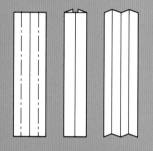

VIEW FROM BACK
(actual size)

STEP 4   Fold each side again using a mountain fold, so that outer edges meet center crease at back. Then adjust folds so that paper looks like an upside-down W, as shown.

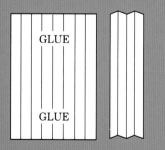

GLUE

GLUE

STEP 5   Unfold fuselage completely. Refold applying glue to all contacting surfaces, as shown. Make sure fuselage is straight.

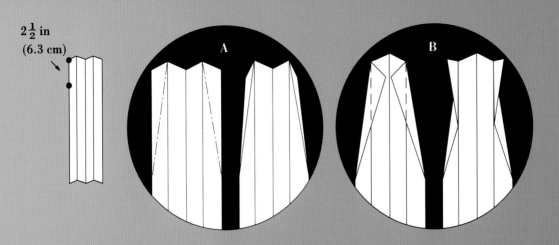

2½ in (6.3 cm)

STEP 6 On each side, measure from top (front of fuselage) and mountain fold along broken lines, as shown in enlarged view A. Then flip over fuselage. On each side, valley fold triangle along broken lines, matching fold line to existing crease, as shown in enlarged view B.

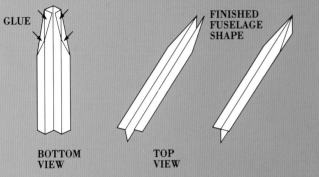

GLUE

BOTTOM VIEW

TOP VIEW

FINISHED FUSELAGE SHAPE

STEP 7 Glue triangles. Hold in place until glue sets. It is important that the fuselage stays straight. Do not glue nose yet.

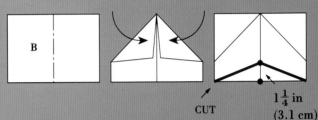

B

CUT

1¼ in (3.1 cm)

STEP 8 Use piece B to make the wings. Lay paper flat in a horizontal direction. Mountain fold in half vertically. Unfold. Then fold each side diagonally so that upper edges meet center crease. Unfold. Measure and cut trailing (back) edge, as shown by heavy line.

AILERONS	ELEVATORS
½ in x ¼ in	¾ in x ¼ in
(1.3 cm x .6 cm)	(1.9 cm x .6 cm)

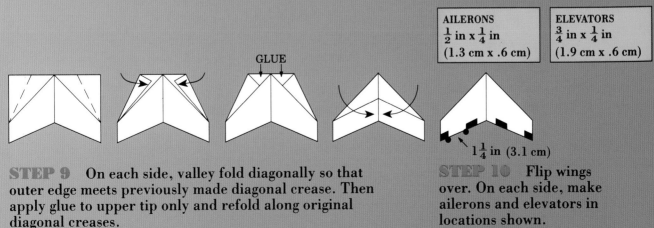

GLUE

1¼ in (3.1 cm)

STEP 9 On each side, valley fold diagonally so that outer edge meets previously made diagonal crease. Then apply glue to upper tip only and refold along original diagonal creases.

STEP 10 Flip wings over. On each side, make ailerons and elevators in locations shown.

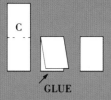

C

GLUE

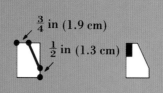

$\frac{3}{4}$ in (1.9 cm)

$\frac{1}{2}$ in (1.3 cm)

RUDDER
$\frac{3}{4}$ in x $\frac{1}{4}$ in
(1.9 cm x .6 cm)

STEP 11   Use piece C to make the vertical tail. Lay paper flat in a vertical direction. Mountain fold in half horizontally. Glue halves together.

STEP 12   Measure and cut, as shown. Make rudder in locations shown.

CANOPY (type 2)
$1\frac{3}{8}$ in x 3 in (3.5 cm x 7.5 cm)
Top point 2 in (5 cm)

D

SLIT
$\frac{1}{2}$ in
(1.3 cm)

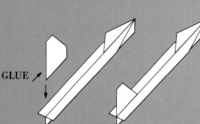

BACK VIEW
(actual size)

E

STEP 13   Use piece D to make the fuselage top. Mountain fold in half horizontally. Unfold. Then valley fold so that the outer edges meet center crease. Unfold. At one end, cut slit along center crease, as indicated by heavy line. Shape folds as shown.

STEP 14   Use piece E to make the canopy. (See p 28).

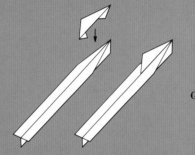

GLUE

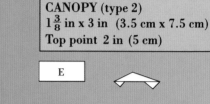

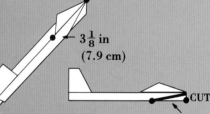

$3\frac{1}{8}$ in
(7.9 cm)

CUT

$2\frac{1}{2}$ in
(6.3 cm)

STEP 15   Apply glue to inside of fuselage at the nose end and insert tabs on the bottom of canopy, aligning at the front. Hold until glue sets.

STEP 16   Apply glue to bottom part of vertical tail and insert into back of fuselage, aligning at the back edge.

STEP 17   Measure from front of fuselage and mark where to position wings. Measure and cut nose, as shown by heavy line.

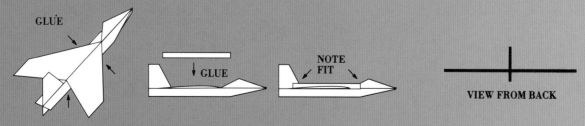

GLUE

GLUE

NOTE
FIT

VIEW FROM BACK

STEP 18   Glue wings to fuselage. Then glue top of fuselage in place so that slit fits around tail and front fits snuggly over back of canopy.

X1 Experimental

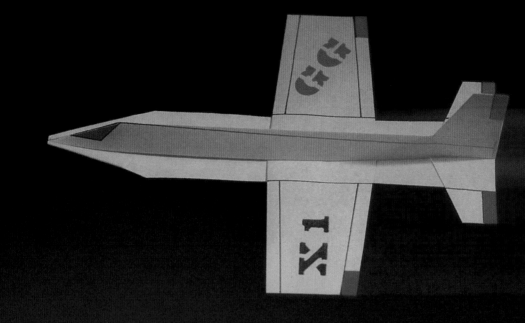

HISTORICAL INFORMATION

Some people believed that the speed of sound was a barrier that would never be crossed. But designers did not abandon their quest. They shaped an airplane like a 50 caliber bullet, which was known to travel faster than the speed of sound. This experimental plane was the stubby-winged Bell X1. It was called "Glamorous Glennis" after the pilot's wife. While this plane did not have swept-back wings, it successfully "broke the sound barrier" for the first time in 1947. Thus began the building of a long series of X planes used for experiments in ultra high speed and high altitude flight. The X15, for example, flew 8 times the speed of sound to the edge of space at an altitude of 70 miles (112 km) in 1956. This paper airplane is modeled on the Bell X1.

Technical Information

Sound Barrier: What we hear as different sounds are actually differences in air pressure that strike our eardrums. These waves of air (called sound waves) travel at about 760 mph. An airplane traveling at that speed creates a tremendous pressure ridge because so many air molecules are piled up ahead of its leading edges. What makes it so dangerous is that as speed increases, the ridge of pressure moves farther back over the wings and begins to affect the control surfaces which are on the trailing edges. Airplanes that successfully fly faster than the speed of sound must be designed so that the pressure is deflected in such a way that it does not affect aircraft control. Thus, their noses are pointed and their wings are thin, and either tapered or swept back. The planes must also be built strong enough to withstand the pressure. When supersonic airplanes break the sound barrier they create a loud booming noise (like a clap of thunder), as heard from the ground.

The speed of sound is also called Mach 1, twice that speed Mach 2, three times Mach 3, and so on, in honor of the scientist Ernst Mach.

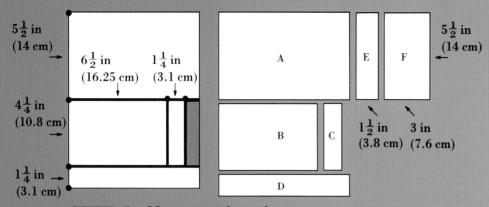

5½ in (14 cm) →

6½ in (16.25 cm) ↓   **1¼ in (3.1 cm)** ↓

4¼ in (10.8 cm) →

1¼ in (3.1 cm) →

A

E   F   **5½ in (14 cm)** ←

B   C

1½ in (3.8 cm)   **3 in (7.6 cm)**

D

STEP 1   Measure and cut the various pieces from a sheet of bond paper, as shown. Two additional pieces E and F are needed, as shown.

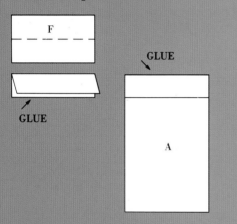

F

GLUE

GLUE

A

STEP 2   Use piece F to make nose ballast. Lay flat in a horizontal direction and valley fold horizontally. Glue halves together. Then glue to piece A, as shown.

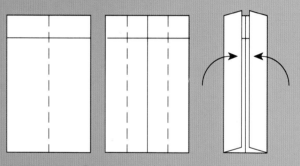

STEP 3   Lay piece A flat in a vertical direction. To make the fuselage, fold in half vertically using a valley fold. Unfold. Then valley fold each side so that outer edges meet center crease, as shown.

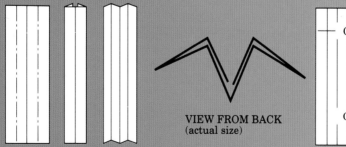

VIEW FROM BACK
(actual size)

STEP 4   Fold each side again using a mountain fold, so that outer edges meet center crease at back. Then adjust folds so that paper looks like an upside-down W, as shown.

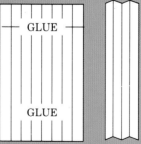

GLUE

GLUE

STEP 5   Unfold fuselage completely. Refold applying glue to all contacting surfaces, as shown. Make sure fuselage is straight.

2 in
(5 cm)

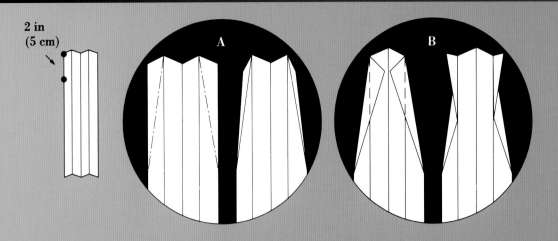

A

B

STEP 6   On each side, measure from top (front of fuselage), mark, and mountain fold along broken lines, as shown in enlarged view A. Then flip over fuselage. On each side, valley fold triangle along broken lines, matching fold line to existing crease, as shown in enlarged view B.

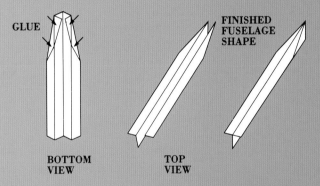

GLUE

FINISHED
FUSELAGE
SHAPE

BOTTOM
VIEW

TOP
VIEW

STEP 7   Glue triangles. Hold in place until glue sets. It is important that the fuselage stays straight. Do not glue nose yet.

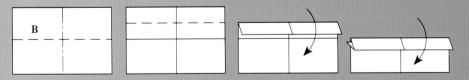

B

STEP 8   Lay piece B horizontally to make the wings. Fold in half horizontally, using a valley fold. Unfold. Fold in half vertically, using a mountain fold. Unfold. Then valley fold so that upper edge meets center crease. Fold over again along original center crease.

GLUE

GLUE

STEP 7 Unfold completely. Refold applying glue to no more than 1 in (2.5) cm) from outer tips, as shown. The folded over part is the bottom of the leading edge (front) of the wings.

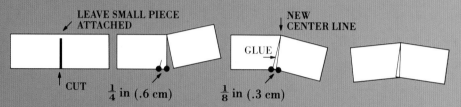

LEAVE SMALL PIECE
ATTACHED

NEW
CENTER LINE

GLUE

CUT $\frac{1}{4}$ in (.6 cm) $\frac{1}{8}$ in (.3 cm)

STEP 8 To taper wings, cut along center heavy line from trailing edge (back), leaving a small piece attached at the leading edge. Then measure and make a mark on trailing edge, as shown. Align pieces to the mark. Glue. Measure and draw a new center line.

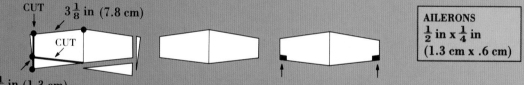

CUT $3\frac{1}{8}$ in (7.8 cm)

CUT

$\frac{1}{2}$ in (1.3 cm)

AILERONS
$\frac{1}{2}$ in x $\frac{1}{4}$ in
(1.3 cm x .6 cm)

STEP 9 On each side, measure and cut, as indicated by heavy lines. On the trailing edges of wingtips, make ailerons.

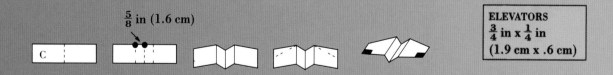

$\frac{5}{8}$ in (1.6 cm)

C

ELEVATORS
$\frac{3}{4}$ in x $\frac{1}{4}$ in
(1.9 cm x .6 cm)

STEP 10 Use piece C to make the horizontal tail. Valley fold in half vertically. Unfold. On each side, measure from center crease, as shown, and mountain fold. On each side, measure and mountain fold leading edge along broken lines. Glue. Make elevators on trailing edges.

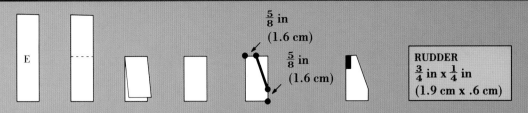

$\frac{5}{8}$ in
(1.6 cm)

$\frac{5}{8}$ in
(1.6 cm)

RUDDER
$\frac{3}{4}$ in x $\frac{1}{4}$ in
(1.9 cm x .6 cm)

STEP 11 Lay piece E vertically to make the vertical tail. Valley fold in half horizontally and glue halves together. Measure and cut along heavy line, as shown. Make rudder on trailing edge.

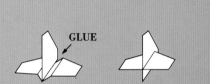

GLUE

CANOPY (type 1)
$1\frac{1}{4}$ in x $8\frac{1}{2}$ in (3.1 cm x 21.7 cm)
Top point $1\frac{1}{2}$ in (3.8 cm)
Back is straight

SLIT $1\frac{1}{4}$ in (3.2 cm)

D

STEP 12 Finish the tail. Apply glue to inside of horizontal tail and slide vertical tail in place, aligning at trailing edge.

STEP 13 Use piece D to make the canopy (see p 28). Make slit in the back of canopy.

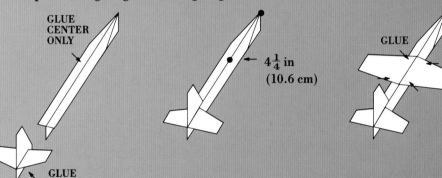

GLUE CENTER ONLY

$4\frac{1}{4}$ in
(10.6 cm)

GLUE

GLUE

STEP 14 Apply glue to inside center only of fuselage. Then apply glue and slide tail into fuselage, aligning at trailing edge. Measure from front and mark for wing position. Glue wings to fuselage.

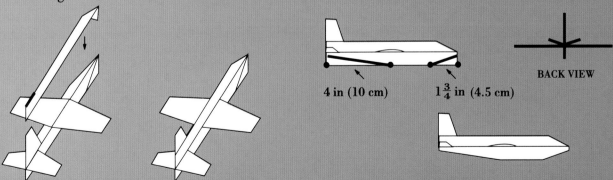

4 in (10 cm)

$1\frac{3}{4}$ in (4.5 cm)

BACK VIEW

STEP 15 Apply glue to inside back of canopy and front tab of canopy. Insert tab into fuselage. The vertical tail fits into slit. Align at nose. To finish, measure and cut front and back of fuselage along heavy diagonal lines, as shown. Adjust dihedral (upward slanting of wings and tail).

Mirage 2000

Technical Information

Delta Wings: The triangle shape of these wings has a unique affect on the air flowing over their upper surfaces. The air flows diagonally towards the fuselage. Like swept-back wings, delta wings prevent the buildup of the pressure ridge created by high speed flight. In addition, the shape lends added stability, and most delta wing airplanes need no additional horizontal stabilizers. However, because they are so stable, some fighter planes have surfaces added to make them less stable and more maneuverable. Delta wings can operate at much greater angles of attack before the air flowing over the top surfaces becomes turbulent and the wings stall.

HISTORICAL INFORMATION

High-speed flight became common after World War II, and wings that swept back came into widespread use because of their efficiency at high speed. Filling in the space between the wingtips of swept-back wings resulted in the formation of triangle shaped wings (delta wings). Delta wings are very stable in flight and are good for supersonic flight. One of their first successful applications was in the early 1950s on the experimental Fairey Delta that exceeded 1000 mph. Two other supersonic planes of the 1950s were the General Dynamics F106 Delta Dart and the Dassault-Breguet Mirage 3. The Mirage has been upgraded several times and is still being built as the Mirage 2000. This paper airplane is modeled on it.

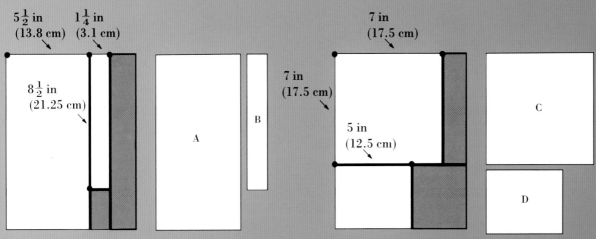

$5\frac{1}{2}$ in (13.8 cm) $1\frac{1}{4}$ in (3.1 cm)

$8\frac{1}{2}$ in (21.25 cm)

A

B

7 in (17.5 cm)

7 in (17.5 cm)

5 in (12.5 cm)

C

D

STEP 1 Measure and cut the various pieces from two sheets of bond paper.

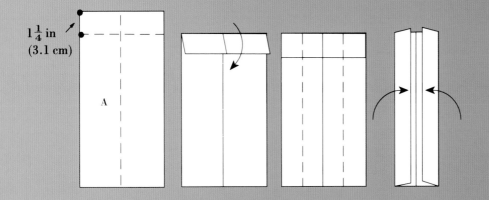

$1\frac{1}{4}$ in (3.1 cm)

A

STEP 2 Lay piece A vertically to make the fuselage. Fold in half vertically using a valley fold. Unfold. Measure from top and valley fold, as shown. Valley fold each side so that outer edges meet center crease, as shown.

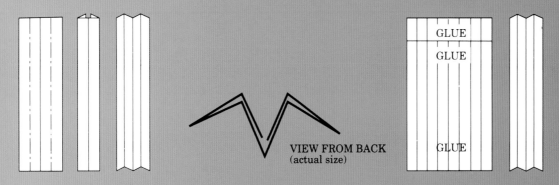

VIEW FROM BACK (actual size)

GLUE
GLUE
GLUE

STEP 3 Fold each side again using a mountain fold, so that outer edges meet center crease at back. Then adjust folds so that paper looks like an upside-down W, as shown.

STEP 4 Unfold fuselage completely. Refold, applying glue to contacting surfaces, as shown. Make sure fuselage is straight.

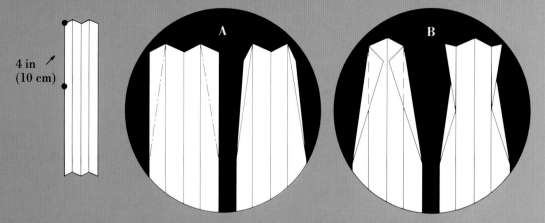

4 in
(10 cm)

A **B**

STEP 5   On each side, measure from top (front of fuselage), mark, and mountain fold along broken lines, as shown in enlarged view A. Then flip over fuselage. On each side, valley fold triangle along broken lines, matching fold line to existing crease, as shown in enlarged view B.

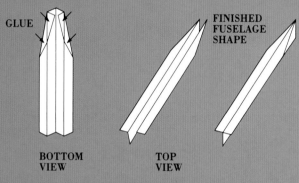

GLUE

FINISHED
FUSELAGE
SHAPE

BOTTOM
VIEW

TOP
VIEW

STEP 6   Glue triangles. Hold in place until glue sets. It is important that the fuselage stays straight. Do not glue nose yet.

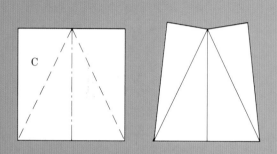

C

STEP 7   Use piece C to make the wings. Mountain fold in half vertically. Unfold. Draw a line from the top center to the lower corners and valley fold along lines, as shown. Unfold.

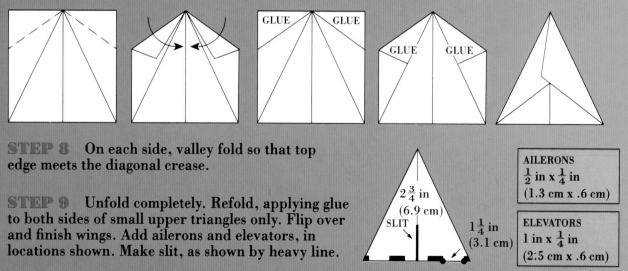

GLUE   GLUE

GLUE   GLUE

STEP 8   On each side, valley fold so that top edge meets the diagonal crease.

STEP 9   Unfold completely. Refold, applying glue to both sides of small upper triangles only. Flip over and finish wings. Add ailerons and elevators, in locations shown. Make slit, as shown by heavy line.

$2\frac{3}{4}$ in
(6.9 cm)

SLIT

$1\frac{1}{4}$ in
(3.1 cm)

AILERONS
$\frac{1}{2}$ in x $\frac{1}{4}$ in
(1.3 cm x .6 cm)

ELEVATORS
1 in x $\frac{1}{4}$ in
(2:5 cm x .6 cm)

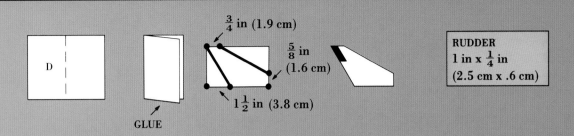

$\frac{3}{4}$ in (1.9 cm)

$\frac{5}{8}$ in (1.6 cm)

$1\frac{1}{2}$ in (3.8 cm)

GLUE

RUDDER
1 in x $\frac{1}{4}$ in
(2.5 cm x .6 cm)

STEP 10 Lay piece D horizontally to make the vertical tail. Valley fold in half vertically. Glue halves together. Turn, as shown, measure, mark, and cut along heavy lines. Make rudder on trailing edge, as shown.

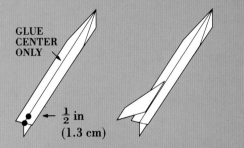

GLUE CENTER ONLY

$\frac{1}{2}$ in (1.3 cm)

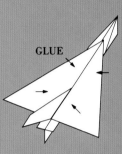

GLUE

STEP 11 Apply glue to inside center only of fuselage. Measure from back of fuselage and mark, as shown. Then apply glue and slide tail into fuselage, aligning at mark.

STEP 12 Apply glue and attach wings to fuselage, slipping around vertical tail. Align trailing edge at the mark.

CANOPY (type 1)
$1\frac{1}{4}$ in x $8\frac{1}{2}$ in (3.1 cm x 21.7 cm)
Top point 3 in (7.5 cm)
Back $\frac{3}{8}$ in (1 cm)

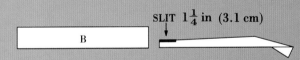

B

SLIT $1\frac{1}{4}$ in (3.1 cm)

STEP 13 Use piece B to make canopy (see p 28). Make a slit at center back of canopy.

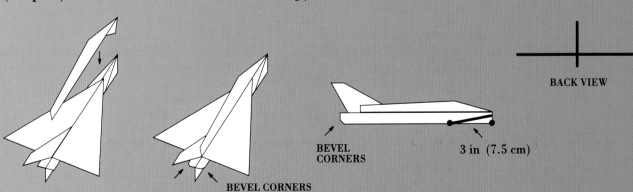

BACK VIEW

BEVEL CORNERS

3 in (7.5 cm)

BEVEL CORNERS

STEP 14 Apply glue to inside back of canopy and front tab of canopy. Insert tab into fuselage. The vertical tail fits into slit. Align at nose. Measure and cut front of fuselage along heavy diagonal line, as shown. To finish, bevel all corners on fuselage back, as shown.

Lifting Body

HISTORICAL INFORMATION

In the 1960s experiments were conducted into designing airplanes with flattened and widened fuselages so that these became lift-producing. This allowed for much smaller wings. Among these planes was the American built X20 Dyna-Soar. Others were the Soviet built Cosmos series of planes, that were actually rocketed into space. All the lifting-body research planes were used to study high speed gliding (therefore the word "soar" in the X20 name). The information gathered was used primarily in developing space vehicles. This paper airplane is modeled on the lifting-body research planes.

Technical Information

Lifting Bodies: The lifting-body research airplanes were not intended for operational use. They were used to demonstrate that wedge-shaped airplanes with very stubby wings could actually fly. Having small wings is important in an airplane that is to be rocketed into space orbit at high speed. Large wings could not stand the stress and would rip off. The angle of attack is very important in the flight of these planes, and is greater than in most airplanes. Because their wings are so small, these planes are roll-unstable. Some experimental planes rocked back and forth wildly in flight. This problem was eventually solved. One successful application of lifting-body research is the Space Shuttle. On its return from space orbit, the shuttle is the world's heaviest and fastest glider.

Making the Lifting Body

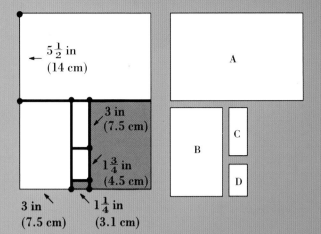

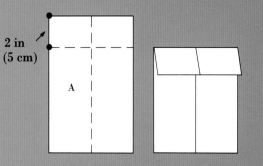

STEP 1 Measure and cut the various pieces from a sheet of bond paper, as shown.

STEP 2 Lay piece A flat in a vertical direction. To make the fuselage, fold in half vertically using a valley fold. Unfold. Measure from top and valley fold, as shown.

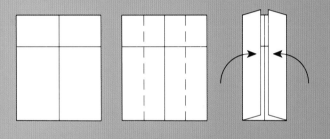

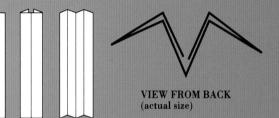

VIEW FROM BACK
(actual size)

STEP 3 Valley fold each side so that outer edges meet center crease, as shown.

STEP 4 Fold each side again using a mountain fold, so that outer edges meet center crease at back. Then adjust folds so that paper looks like an upside-down W, as shown.

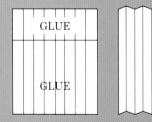

STEP 5 Unfold fuselage completely. Refold applying glue to all contacting surfaces, as shown. Make sure fuselage is straight.

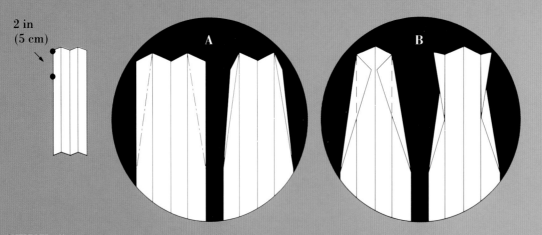

2 in
(5 cm)

STEP 6 On each side, measure from top (front of fuselage), mark, and mountain fold along broken lines, as shown in enlarged view A. Then flip over fuselage. On each side, valley fold triangle along broken lines, matching fold line to existing crease, as shown in enlarged view B.

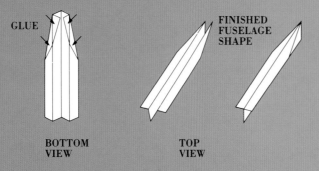

GLUE

FINISHED FUSELAGE SHAPE

BOTTOM VIEW

TOP VIEW

STEP 7 Glue triangles. Hold in place until glue sets. It is important that the fuselage stays straight. Do not glue nose yet.

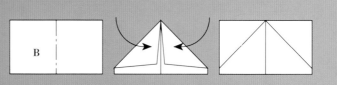

B

STEP 8 Use piece B to make the wings. Lay paper flat in a horizontal direction. Mountain fold in half vertically. Unfold. Then fold each side diagonally so that upper edges meet center crease. Unfold.

RUDDERS $\frac{3}{8}$ in x $\frac{1}{4}$ in (1 cm x .6 cm)	AILERONS $\frac{3}{8}$ in x $\frac{1}{4}$ in (1 cm x .6 cm)	ELEVATORS $\frac{3}{8}$ in x $\frac{1}{4}$ in (1 cm x .6 cm)

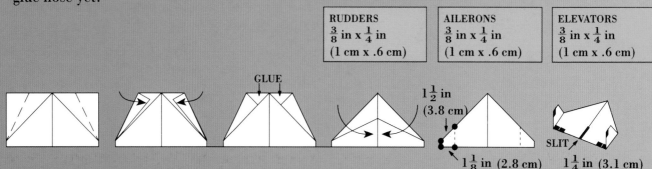

GLUE

$1\frac{1}{2}$ in (3.8 cm)

$1\frac{1}{8}$ in (2.8 cm)

SLIT

$1\frac{1}{4}$ in (3.1 cm)

STEP 9 On each side, valley fold diagonally so that outer edge meets previously made diagonal crease. Then apply glue to upper tip only and refold along original diagonal creases. Flip wings over. On each side, measure and valley fold wingtips to make vertical tails.

STEP 10 Make a slit at the center back of wings, as shown. Make rudders, ailerons, and elevators in locations shown.

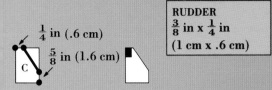

$\frac{1}{4}$ in (.6 cm)

$\frac{5}{8}$ in (1.6 cm)

C

RUDDER
$\frac{3}{8}$ in x $\frac{1}{4}$ in
(1 cm x .6 cm)

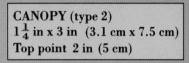

CANOPY (type 2)
$1\frac{1}{4}$ in x 3 in (3.1 cm x 7.5 cm)
Top point 2 in (5 cm)

D

STEP 11   Use piece C to make a center vertical tail. Measure and cut, as shown. Make rudder in location shown.

STEP 12   Use piece D to make the canopy. (See p 28).

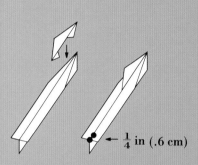

$\frac{1}{4}$ in (.6 cm)

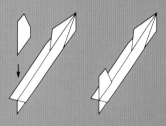

STEP 13   Applying glue to inside of fuselage at the nose end, insert tabs on the bottom of canopy, aligning at front. Measure from back of fuselage and mark wing position.

STEP 14   Applying glue to bottom part of vertical tail, insert into back of fuselage, aligning at back edge.

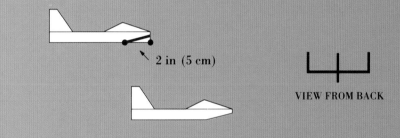

2 in (5 cm)

VIEW FROM BACK

STEP 15   Glue wings to fuselage. Align trailing (back) edge to the mark so that slit fits around center vertical tail.

STEP 16   Measure from front of fuselage and cut nose, as shown by heavy diagonal line. Adjust vertical tails to be vertical.

Glider

HISTORICAL INFORMATION

While Wilber Wright was mainly interested in powered flight, his brother Orville experimented with gliders. Both types of flight continued to be developed. By the time World War II ended much had been learned about good aerodynamic performance. During the 1950s and 60s the design of gliders was greatly improved as builders produced low-drag gliders with highly efficient wings. With long soaring flights now possible, Orville's dream of sustained motorless flight was fulfilled. In Europe, Germany became well known for its gliders. In the USA, the Schweizer brothers of New York built good training gliders that did much to promote gliding in North America. Soaring became a popular sport the world over. This paper airplane is modeled on gliders.

Technical Information

Aspect Ratio: Wings that are short, like the ones foun on the X1 and the Lifting Body, have a low aspect rat Wings that are long and slender have a high aspect rat Wings with a high aspect ratio produce more lift for t amount of drag they create. This makes them suitable for gliders, where the smallest amount of drag possibl is best. Today's gliders are very efficient. They soar li the eagles. From an altitude of 6000 ft (1800 m) som of them can fly about 60 nautical miles forward witho any additional lift. To gain altitude, pilots usually take advantage of columns of rising air. (This is air that ha been warmed by the ground on a sunny day, making i lighter and consequently making it rise.) Some glider pilots have remained airborne for more than ten hour and flown distances of more than 1000 nautical miles without landing. They have reached altitudes of more than 40,000 ft (12,000 m). Because the columns of rising air are invisible, it takes skill, and sometimes luc to find and stay in them. Many countries have nationa gliding competitions where the best pilots demonstrate their skills.

Making the Glider

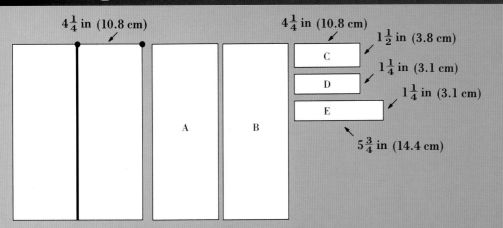

4¼ in (10.8 cm)

4¼ in (10.8 cm)

1½ in (3.8 cm)

C

1¼ in (3.1 cm)

D

1¼ in (3.1 cm)

E

5¾ in (14.4 cm)

A   B

STEP 1   Measure and cut a sheet of bond paper, as shown. Three additional pieces are needed, as shown.

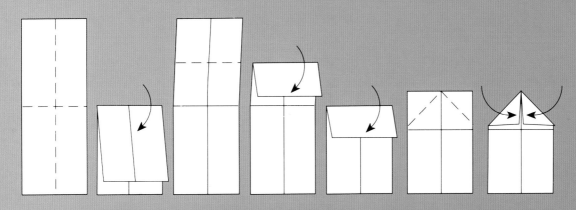

STEP 2   To make the fuselage, fold piece A in half vertically using a valley fold. Unfold. Valley fold in half horizontally. Unfold. Then valley fold so that upper edge meets horizontal crease. Refold original horizontal crease. Then on each side, valley fold diagonally so that top edge meets center crease.

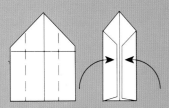

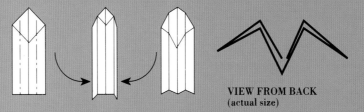

VIEW FROM BACK
(actual size)

STEP 3   Valley fold each side so that outer edges meet center crease, as shown.

STEP 4   Fold again using a mountain fold, so that outer edges meet center crease at back. Then adjust folds so that paper looks like an upside-down W, as shown.

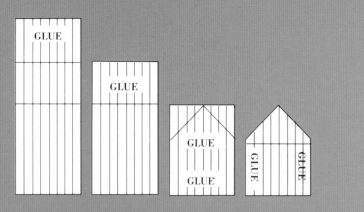

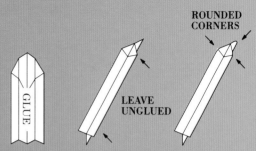

STEP 5 Unfold fuselage completely. Refold, applying glue to contacting surfaces, as shown. Make sure fuselage is straight.

STEP 6 Glue center of fuselage, leaving 1 in (2.5 cm) at the nose and 1 in (2.5 cm) at the tail end unglued. Round corners at nose end.

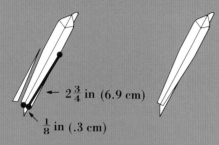

$2\frac{3}{4}$ in (6.9 cm)

$\frac{1}{8}$ in (.3 cm)

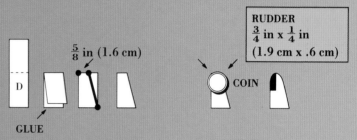

$\frac{5}{8}$ in (1.6 cm)

D

GLUE

RUDDER
$\frac{3}{4}$ in x $\frac{1}{4}$ in
(1.9 cm x .6 cm)

COIN

STEP 7 On each side, measure and cut fuselage back, as shown by heavy lines.

STEP 8 Lay piece D vertically to make the vertical tail. Valley fold in half horizontally. Glue halves together. Measure and cut leading edge along heavy line, as shown. Trace around a coin and cut out to round corners (see p 26). On trailing edge, make rudder.

$\frac{1}{2}$ in (1.3 cm)

C

$\frac{3}{4}$ in (1.9 cm)

STEP 9 Use piece C to make the horizontal tail. Valley fold in half vertically. Unfold. On each side, measure from center crease, as shown, and mountain fold. On each side, measure and cut leading edges along heavy lines, as shown.

COIN

ELEVATORS
$1\frac{1}{4}$ in x $\frac{1}{4}$ in
(3.1 cm x .6 cm)

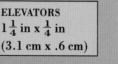

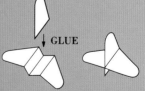

GLUE

STEP 10 Trace around a coin and cut out to make all the corners rounded (see p 26). On trailing edges, make elevators.

STEP 11 Apply glue to inside of horizontal tail and insert vertical tail, aligning trailing edges.

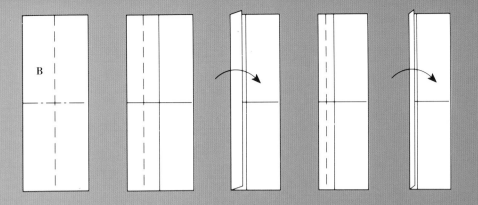

STEP 12 Use piece B to make the wings. Fold in half horizontally, using a mountain fold. Unfold. Fold in half vertically, using a valley fold. Unfold. Then valley fold so that outer edge meets center crease. Fold same side again so that outer edge again meets center crease. Refold original horizontal center crease.

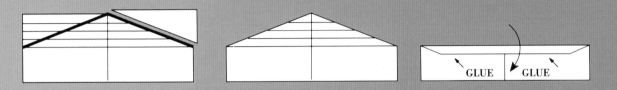

STEP 13 Unfold completely. On each side, draw and cut diagonally along heavy lines, as shown. Refold. Apply glue before refolding original horizontal center crease only. The folded over part is the bottom of the leading edge (front) of the wings. These slender wings are quite fragile. When they are completed, make sure they are not twisted.

STEP 14 Measure and cut trailing edge (back) of wings, as shown by heavy lines. Then trace around a coin and cut out to make rounded corners at both leading edges and trailing edges, as shown (see p 26).

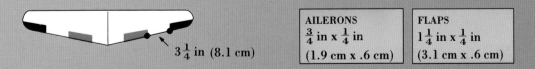

AILERONS	FLAPS
$\frac{3}{4}$ in x $\frac{1}{4}$ in	$1\frac{1}{4}$ in x $\frac{1}{4}$ in
(1.9 cm x .6 cm)	(3.1 cm x .6 cm)

STEP 15 At wingtips on trailing edges, make ailerons. Then make secondary control surfaces (flaps), in locations shown.

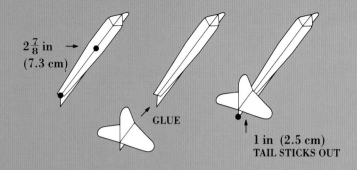

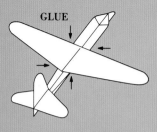

$2\frac{7}{8}$ in
(7.3 cm)

GLUE

1 in (2.5 cm)
TAIL STICKS OUT

GLUE

STEP 16 Measure from back of fuselage and mark position of leading edge (front) of wing. Apply glue and slide tail into back of fuselage.

STEP 17 At the mark, attach wings to fuselage.

CANOPY (type 1)
$1\frac{1}{4}$ in x $5\frac{3}{4}$ in (3.1 cm x 14.6 cm)
Top point 1 in (2.5 cm)
Back $\frac{1}{4}$ in (.6 cm)

SLIT $\frac{3}{4}$ in (1.9 cm)

← ROUNDED TOP POINT

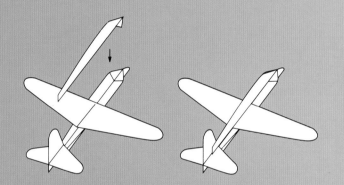

STEP 18 Make the canopy, using piece E (see p 28). Make a slit at the center back, as shown. Round the top point slightly.

STEP 19 Apply glue to inside back and front tab of canopy. Insert tab into fuselage, sliding vertical tail into slit. Align at nose.

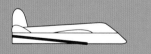

VIEW FROM BACK

STEP 20 Measure and cut back of fuselage along heavy diagonal line, as shown. Adjust dihedral (upward slanting of wings and tail), as shown.

F16 Falcon

HISTORICAL INFORMATION

In the early 1970s the General Dynamics F16 was an experimental airplane used to test new lightweight materials and computer technology. Since then it has become one of the most maneuverable and versatile fighter planes ever made, and is used for a wide range of military tasks. It can be found in the air forces of at least ten countries. Its ailerons, elevators, and rudder, as well as navigation and weapons systems, are controlled by computer. The plane has modified delta wings with a conventional tail. For added stability it has a pair of canted (slanted) ventral fins beneath the horizontal stabilizers. It is commonly called the "Falcon". This paper airplane in modeled on the F16.

Technical Information

The F16 has a flattened fuselage, something like a lifting body. While the wings of this plane are basically triangular, they attach to the fuselage with extensions on the leading edges called strakes. They improve the flight characteristics of the plane at very low and very high speeds. In this paper model the flattened fuselage acts as part of the leading edge extensions. The F16 has a single turbojet engine with an afterburner and can fly twice the speed of sound at an altitude of 60,000 ft (18,000 m). Its air intake is situated in line with the canopy underneath the fuselage. The F16 has much improved fuel efficiency over older jet fighters. It has a missile rail at each wingtip, and can carry extra fuel tanks as well as a variety of armament under the wings. This makes it useful for both air-to-air and air-to-ground military operations. Besides its military role, this aircraft is also used as an aerial display plane at air shows.

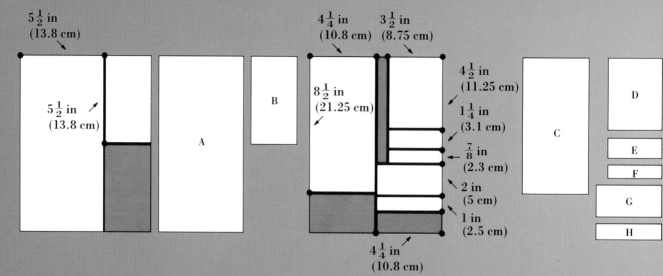

5 1/2 in (13.8 cm)

5 1/2 in (13.8 cm)

A

B

4 1/4 in (10.8 cm)

3 1/2 in (8.75 cm)

8 1/2 in (21.25 cm)

4 1/2 in (11.25 cm)

1 1/4 in (3.1 cm)

7/8 in (2.3 cm)

2 in (5 cm)

1 in (2.5 cm)

4 1/4 in (10.8 cm)

C

D

E

F

G

H

STEP 1 Measure and cut the various pieces from two sheets of bond paper, as shown.

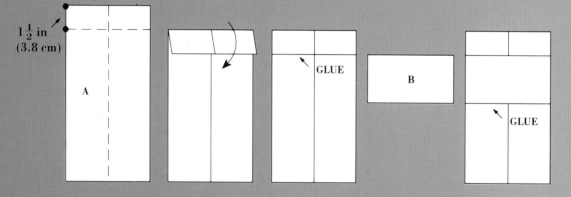

1 1/2 in (3.8 cm)

A

GLUE

B

GLUE

STEP 2 Lay piece A flat in a vertical direction. To make the fuselage, fold in half vertically using a valley fold. Unfold. Measure and valley fold horizontally, as shown. Glue this flap down. Then glue piece B in place, aligning against the glued-down flap, as shown.

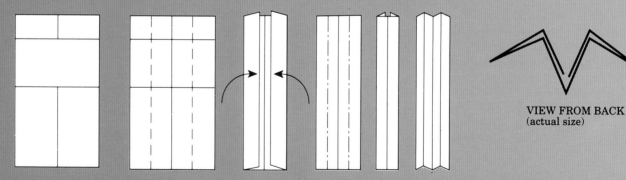

VIEW FROM BACK (actual size)

STEP 3 Refold in half vertically using a valley fold. Unfold. Valley fold each side so that the outer edges meet center crease, as shown. Fold each side again using a mountain fold, so that outer edges meet center crease at back. Then adjust folds so that paper looks like an upside-down W, as shown.

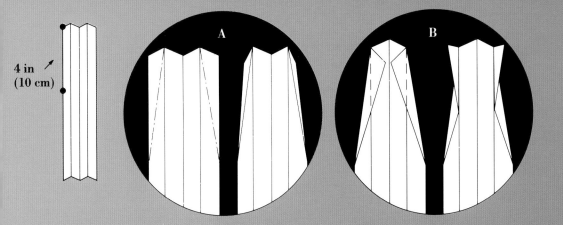

4 in
(10 cm)

STEP 4   On each side, measure from top (front of fuselage), mark, and mountain fold along broken lines, as shown in enlarged view A. Then flip over fuselage. On each side, valley fold triangle along broken lines, matching fold line to existing crease, as shown in enlarged view B.

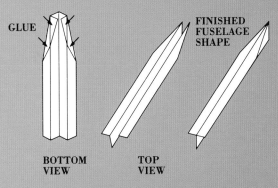

GLUE

FINISHED
FUSELAGE
SHAPE

BOTTOM
VIEW

TOP
VIEW

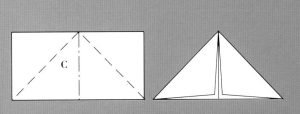

C

STEP 5   Glue triangles. Hold in place until glue sets. It is important that the fuselage stays straight. Do not glue nose yet.

STEP 6   Use piece C to make the wings. Fold in half vertically, using a mountain fold. Unfold. On each side, valley fold diagonally so that top edge meets center crease, as shown.

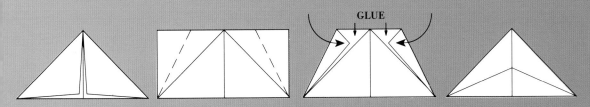

GLUE

STEP 7   Unfold diagonal folds. On each side, valley fold diagonally so that outer edges meet diagonal crease, as shown. Apply glue to small upper triangles only and refold original diagonal creases.

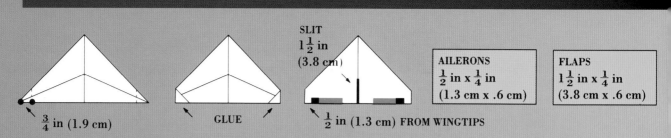

SLIT
$1\frac{1}{2}$ in
(3.8 cm)

$\frac{3}{4}$ in (1.9 cm) GLUE $\frac{1}{2}$ in (1.3 cm) FROM WINGTIPS

AILERONS
$\frac{1}{2}$ in x $\frac{1}{4}$ in
(1.3 cm x .6 cm)

FLAPS
$1\frac{1}{2}$ in x $\frac{1}{4}$ in
(3.8 cm x .6 cm)

STEP 8 At each wingtip, measure and valley fold, as shown. Glue down the small triangles. Flip over and make ailerons and flaps in locations shown. At the trailing edge, make a slit along the center crease.

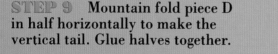

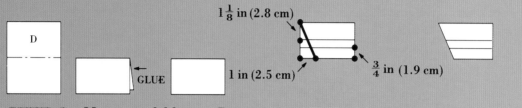

D

GLUE

$1\frac{1}{8}$ in (2.8 cm)

1 in (2.5 cm) $\frac{3}{4}$ in (1.9 cm)

STEP 9 Mountain fold piece D in half horizontally to make the vertical tail. Glue halves together.

STEP 10 Measure and draw lines, as shown. Cut diagonally, as shown by heavy lines.

ELEVATORS
$1\frac{3}{8}$ in x $\frac{3}{8}$ in
(3.5 cm x 1 cm)

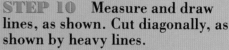

$\frac{7}{8}$ in (2.3 cm)
1 in (2.5 cm)

RUDDER
$1\frac{1}{4}$ in x $\frac{1}{4}$ in
(3.1 cm x .6 cm)

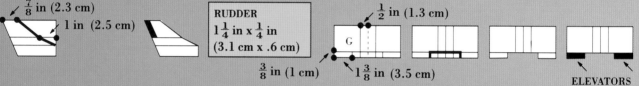

$\frac{1}{2}$ in (1.3 cm)

G

$\frac{3}{8}$ in (1 cm) $1\frac{3}{8}$ in (3.5 cm)

ELEVATORS

STEP 11 Measure and draw additional lines to make leading edge, as shown. Cut diagonally, as shown by heavy lines. Add rudder.

STEP 12 Use piece G to make horizontal tail. Valley fold in half vertically. Unfold. On each side, measure and draw lines. To make elevators, cut out piece, as shown by heavy lines.

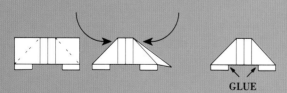

GLUE

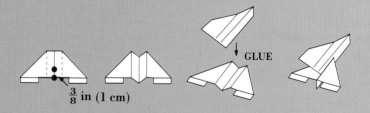

GLUE

$\frac{3}{8}$ in (1 cm)

STEP 13 On each side, mountain fold diagonally so that upper edge meets vertical crease, as shown. Glue.

STEP 14 Measure from back and make a mark. On each side, mountain fold along lines, as shown. Apply glue to inside of horizontal tail and isert vertical tail, aligning trailing edge (back) to the mark.

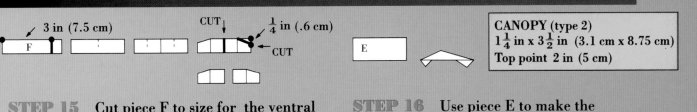

3 in (7.5 cm)   F

CUT $\frac{1}{4}$ in (.6 cm)   CUT

E

CANOPY (type 2)
$1\frac{1}{4}$ in x $3\frac{1}{2}$ in (3.1 cm x 8.75 cm)
Top point 2 in (5 cm)

STEP 15 Cut piece F to size for the ventral fins, as shown. Mountain fold in half vertically. Unfold. On each side, mountain fold in half vertically so that outer edge meets center crease. Unfold. On each side, measure and cut, as shown by heavy line. Then cut in two along center crease.

STEP 16 Use piece E to make the canopy. (See p 28.)

STEP 17 Measure from front of fuselage and make marks for positioning the leading edges of canopy at I, wings at J, ventral fins at K.

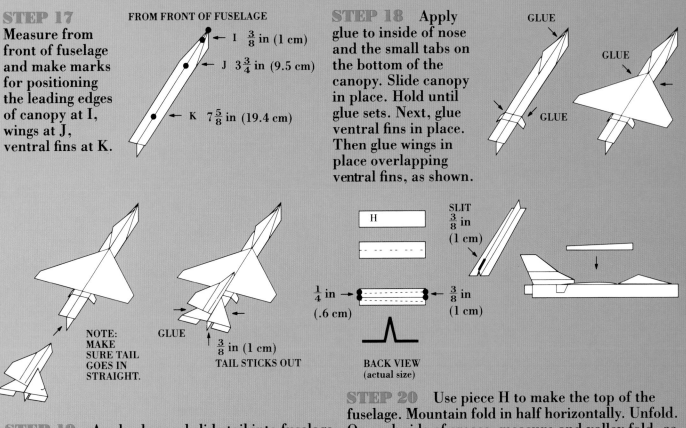

FROM FRONT OF FUSELAGE

I $\frac{3}{8}$ in (1 cm)

J $3\frac{3}{4}$ in (9.5 cm)

K $7\frac{5}{8}$ in (19.4 cm)

STEP 18 Apply glue to inside of nose and the small tabs on the bottom of the canopy. Slide canopy in place. Hold until glue sets. Next, glue ventral fins in place. Then glue wings in place overlapping ventral fins, as shown.

GLUE   GLUE   GLUE

NOTE: MAKE SURE TAIL GOES IN STRAIGHT.

GLUE $\frac{3}{8}$ in (1 cm)   TAIL STICKS OUT

H

SLIT $\frac{3}{8}$ in (1 cm)

$\frac{1}{4}$ in (.6 cm) $\frac{3}{8}$ in (1 cm)

BACK VIEW (actual size)

STEP 19 Apply glue and slide tail into fuselage. The tail sticks out of the back end of fuselage, with the vertical tail sliding into slit in the wings.

STEP 20 Use piece H to make the top of the fuselage. Mountain fold in half horizontally. Unfold. On each side of crease, measure and valley fold, as shown. Make slit. Glue onto top of fuselage, as shown. The vertical tail slides into slit. Fit the front snuggly over back of canopy.

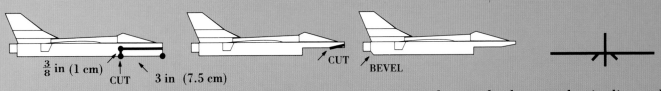

$\frac{3}{8}$ in (1 cm)   CUT   3 in (7.5 cm)   CUT   BEVEL

STEP 21 Measure and cut nose, as shown. First cut a rectangular notch, then cut the tip diagonally to give final shape to the nose. Bevel back of fuselage. This plane has no dihedral. Ventral fins are canted (slanted) 45°.

F18 Hornet

Technical Information

The F18 is constructed mostly of aluminum, with part of its wings and other surfaces made of composites. It has two afterburning turbojet engines that can propel i at almost twice the speed of sound when traveling at high altitude. This airplane is both a fighter and an attack plane, and it can be fitted with a wide variety of armament for both air-to-air and air-to-ground military tasks. Like the F16, it has a missile rail at each wingtip with space under the wings for other armament and extra fuel tanks. Besides its military role, this plane is also used as an aerial display airplane at air shows.

HISTORICAL INFORMATION

The F16 was used as a land-based fighter aircraft but there was no equivalent sea-based fighter. Therefore the F18 was built in the early 1980s as a medium sized multi-task maneuverable military aircraft capable of both sea and land operations. This plane is commonly called the "Hornet." It has tapered wings and a conventional horizontal tail, but with two canted (tilted) vertical tails located between the wings and horizontal tail. The F18 is used by the USA, Canada, Australia, and Spain. This paper airplane is modeled on the F18.

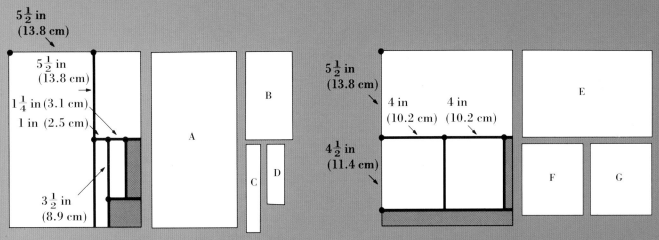

STEP 1   Measure and cut the various pieces from two sheets of bond paper.

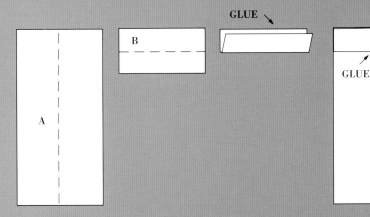

STEP 2   Use piece A to make the fuselage. Fold in half vertically using a valley fold. Unfold. Then valley fold piece B in half horizontally to make nose ballast. Glue halves together. Glue B to A, aligning top edges, as shown.

STEP 3   Valley fold so that outer edges meet center crease.

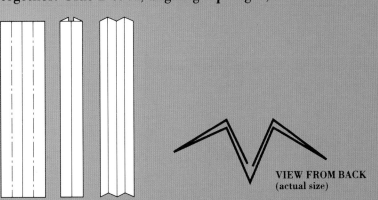

STEP 4   Fold each side again using a mountain fold, so that outer edges meet center crease at back. Then adjust folds so that paper looks like an upside-down W, as shown.

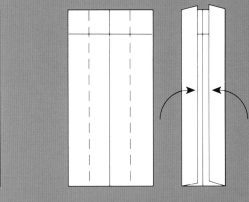

STEP 5   Unfold fuselage completely. Refold applying glue to contacting surfaces, as shown. Make sure fuselage is straight.

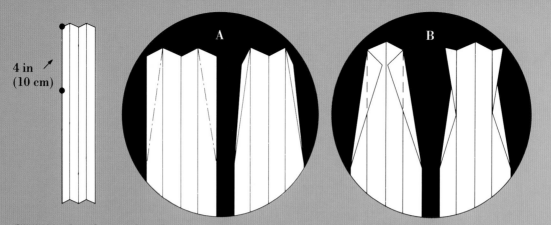

4 in (10 cm)

A

B

STEP 6 On each side, measure from top (front of fuselage), mark, and mountain fold along broken lines, as shown in enlarged view A. Then flip over fuselage. On each side, valley fold the triangle along the broken lines, matching fold line to existing crease, as shown in enlarged view B.

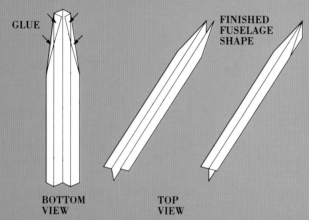

GLUE

FINISHED FUSELAGE SHAPE

BOTTOM VIEW

TOP VIEW

STEP 7 Glue triangles. Hold in place until glue sets. It is important that the fuselage stays straight. Do not glue nose yet.

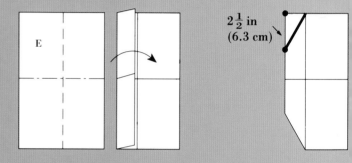

E

2½ in (6.3 cm)

STEP 8 Lay piece E in a vertical direction to make wings. Valley fold in half vertically. Unfold. Mountain fold in half horizontally. Valley fold so that one outer edge meets center crease, as shown. On each side of horizontal center crease, measure and cut diagonally, as shown by heavy line.

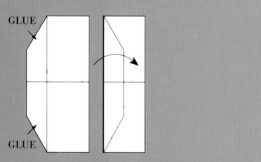

GLUE

GLUE

STEP 9 Apply glue to each diagonal side on top layer only, no more than 1 in (2.5 cm) from the diagonal edge. Refold along the original vertical center crease. The folded-over part is the bottom of the leading edge (front) of wings.

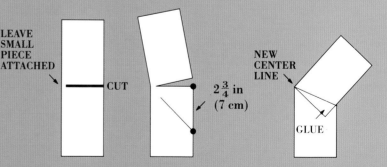

LEAVE SMALL PIECE ATTACHED

CUT

2¾ in (7 cm)

NEW CENTER LINE

GLUE

STEP 10 To taper wings, cut along center line from the trailing edge (back), leaving a small piece attached at the leading edge. Then measure and draw diagonal line, as shown. Align halves to the diagonal line. Glue. Draw new center line.

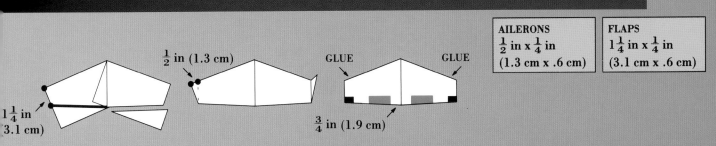

STEP 11 On each side, measure and cut trailing edge, as shown by heavy line. Then on each side, measure and mountain fold wingtips. Glue. Make ailerons and flaps in locations shown.

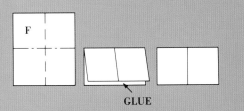

STEP 12 Lay piece F flat in a vertical direction to make the horizontal tail. Valley fold in half vertically. Unfold. Mountain fold in half horizontally. Glue halves together.

STEP 13 On each side, measure and cut, as shown by heavy lines. Make elevators.

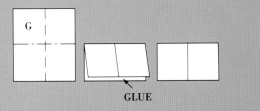

STEP 14 Lay piece G flat in a vertical direction to make the twin vertical tails. Valley fold in half vertically. Unfold. Mountain fold in half horizontally. Glue halves together.

STEP 15 On each side, measure and cut, as shown by heavy lines. Make a rudder on each vertical tail. On each side, valley fold, as shown.

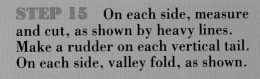

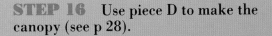

STEP 16 Use piece D to make the canopy (see p 28).

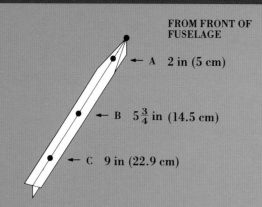

FROM FRONT OF
FUSELAGE

← A 2 in (5 cm)

← B $5\frac{3}{4}$ in (14.5 cm)

← C 9 in (22.9 cm)

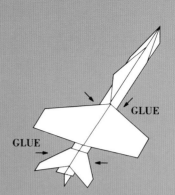

GLUE

GLUE

STEP 17 Measure from front of fuselage, as shown, and make mark A for positioning the front of the canopy, mark B for positioning leading edge of the wings, and mark C for positioning leading edge of the horizontal tail.

STEP 18 Apply glue to the inside of the nose and the small triangles on the bottom of the canopy. Position canopy on the fuselage at mark A. Hold until glue sets. Glue wings and horizontal tail in place, making sure they are centered and at right angles to the fuselage.

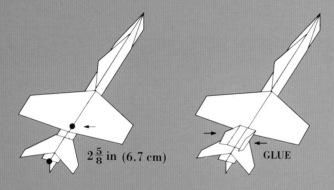

$2\frac{5}{8}$ in (6.7 cm)

GLUE

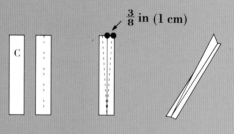

$\frac{3}{8}$ in (1 cm)

C

STEP 19 Measure from back of fuselage, as shown, and make a mark for positioning the twin vertical tails. Glue vertical tails in place, making sure they are centered and parallel to the fuselage.

STEP 20 Lay piece C in a vertical direction to make the fuselage top. Mountain fold in half vertically. Unfold. On each side, measure and valley fold. Adjust shape, as shown.

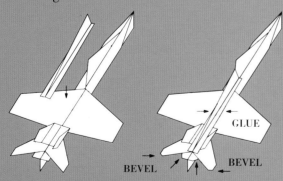

BEVEL

GLUE

BEVEL

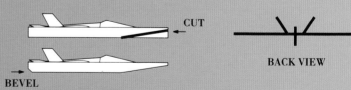

CUT

BEVEL

BACK VIEW

STEP 21 Glue piece C onto the fuselage, making sure it fits snugly against the canopy. Bevel the trailing edges of the elevators.

STEP 22 Measure and cut nose diagonally, as shown by heavy line. Bevel all corners of the back of the fuselage. Wings and horizontal tail are level. Adjust angles of the canted (tilted) vertical tails, as shown.

747 Jumbo

HISTORICAL INFORMATION

The first jet-powered airliner was the deHavilland Comet built in the 1950s. As more and more people realized the comfort of jet travel, bigger airplanes were needed to carry them. The Boeing 747 was first built in 1968. It is one of the largest passenger-carrying airplanes in the world. It is longer than the distance flown by the Wright brothers (120 ft or 36 m)) in their first powered flight. The "Jumbo Jet" is used to carry passengers and cargo across the continents and the oceans of the world. This paper airplane is modeled on the 747.

Technical Information

The Boeing 747 is a big airplane. From nose to tail it measures 230 ft (69 m). The distance from wingtip to wingtip is 195 ft (58.5 m). Its tail is 64 ft (19 m) high, higher than a five storey building. When it is fully loaded with fuel, passengers, and cargo, it weighs 800,000 lb (360,000 kg), and carries 500 passengers or 270,000 lb (121,500 kg) of cargo. Once it reaches high altitude, it cruises at 600 mph (960 km/h). This makes it ideal for use on long-distance passenger routes. Its service ceiling is 40,000 ft (12,000 m) above the ground. Its maximum range is 6000 miles (9600 km), allowing it to fly one fourth of the distance around the earth without refueling. The plane is propelled by four 50,000 lb thrust turbofan jet engines.

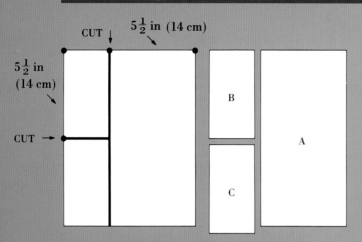

STEP 1 Measure and cut three pieces from a sheet of bond paper, as shown.

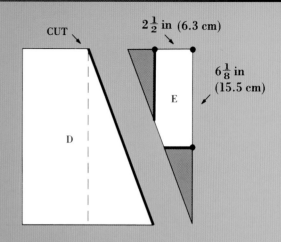

STEP 2 Valley fold a second sheet of bond paper in half vertically. Then measure and cut two pieces, as shown.

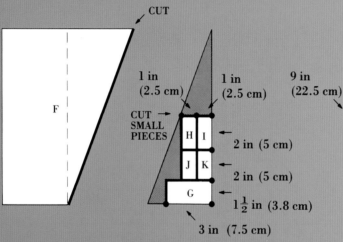

STEP 3 Valley fold a third sheet of bond paper in half vertically. Then measure and cut six pieces, as shown.

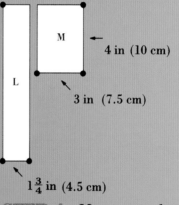

STEP 4 Measure and cut two additional pieces, as shown.

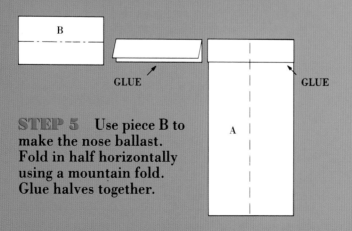

STEP 5 Use piece B to make the nose ballast. Fold in half horizontally using a mountain fold. Glue halves together.

STEP 6 Use piece A to make the fuselage. Glue ballast to the top of fuselage, as shown. Fold in half vertically using a valley fold. Unfold.

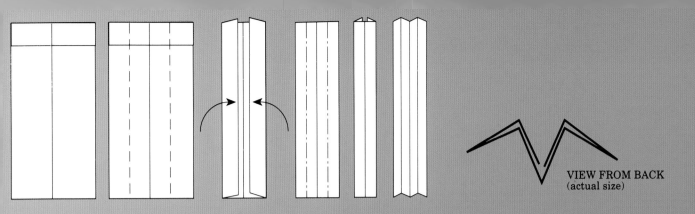

VIEW FROM BACK
(actual size)

STEP 7   Valley fold each side so that outer edges meet center crease, as shown.

STEP 8   Fold each side again using a mountain fold, so that outer edges meet center crease at back. Then adjust folds so that paper looks like an upside-down W, as shown.

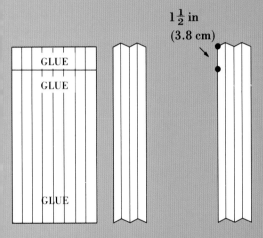

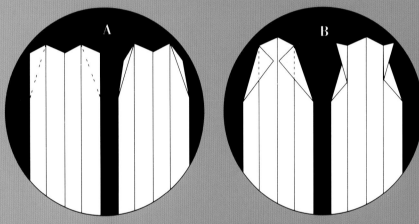

$1\frac{1}{2}$ in
(3.8 cm)

STEP 9   Unfold fuselage completely. Refold applying glue to contacting surfaces, as shown. Make sure fuselage is straight.

STEP 10   On each side, measure from top (front of fuselage), mark, and mountain fold along broken lines, as shown in enlarged view A. Then flip over fuselage. On each side, valley fold triangle along broken lines, matching fold line to existing crease, as shown in enlarged view B.

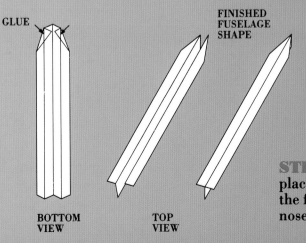

GLUE

FINISHED
FUSELAGE
SHAPE

BOTTOM
VIEW

TOP
VIEW

STEP 11   Glue triangles. Hold in place until glue sets. It is important that the fuselage stays straight. Do not glue nose yet.

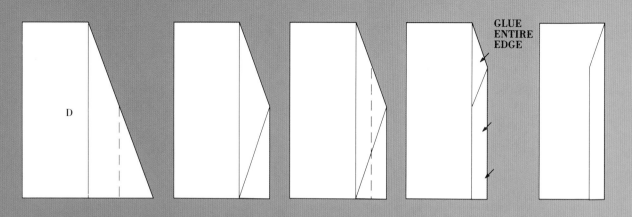

GLUE
ENTIRE
EDGE

STEP 12 Lay piece D vertically to make the right wing. Valley fold vertically so that bottom outer edge meets center crease. Valley fold vertically again so that outer edge meets center crease. Apply glue. Then fold over again along original vertical center crease.

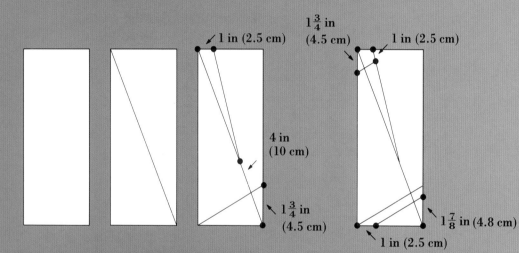

$1\frac{3}{4}$ in (4.5 cm)

1 in (2.5 cm)

1 in (2.5 cm)

4 in (10 cm)

$1\frac{3}{4}$ in (4.5 cm)

$1\frac{7}{8}$ in (4.8 cm)

1 in (2.5 cm)

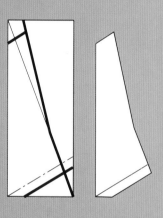

STEP 13 Flip over, with folded-over edge to the LEFT. Draw diagonal line from upper left to lower right corners. Measure along line from bottom and make a mark. Measure along top edge from left and mark. Join the two marks. Then measure along right edge from bottom and mark. Join this point with the bottom left corner.

STEP 14 Measure along left edge from top and make a mark. Measure along line from top, as shown, and make a mark. Join the two marks. Then measure along bottom edge from left and make mark. Measure along right edge from bottom and make a mark. Join marks.

STEP 15 Cut along heavy lines, as shown. Then mountain fold along line, as shown.

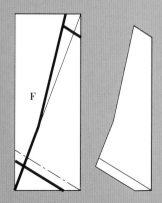

F

STEP 16 To make the left wing, repeat steps 12-15 using piece F, keeping the folded edge on the RIGHT and reversing the directions of the lines from left to right, as shown.

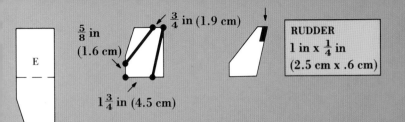

RUDDER
1 in x $\frac{1}{4}$ in
(2.5 cm x .6 cm)

STEP 17 Lay piece E vertically to make the vertical tail. Valley fold in half horizontally and glue halves together. Then cut along heavy lines, as shown. Make rudder on trailing edge.

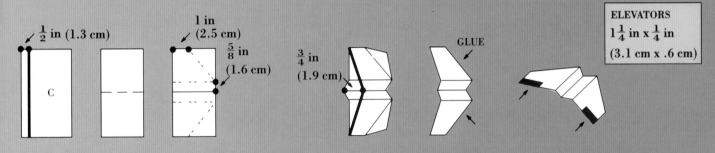

ELEVATORS
1$\frac{1}{4}$ in x $\frac{1}{4}$ in
(3.1 cm x .6 cm)

STEP 18 Lay piece C vertically to make the horizontal tail. Measure and cut to size. Valley fold in half horizontally. Unfold. On each side, measure from center crease, as shown, and mountain fold. On each side, measure and mountain fold leading edge along broken lines. Glue. Cut trailing edges and make elevators.

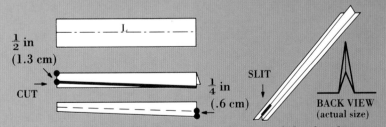

CANOPY (Modified type 2)
1 in x 3 in (2.5 cm x 7.5 cm)
with top points 1$\frac{1}{4}$ in (3.1 cm)
from front and back tips

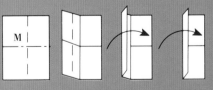

GLUE

STEP 19 Apply glue to inside of horizontal tail and insert vertical tail, aligning leading (front) edges.

STEP 20 Use piece G to make the canopy (see p 28). Use pieces H, I, J, and K to make the engines. Wrap each piece around a pencil vertically and glue.

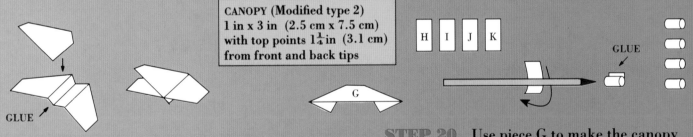

STEP 21 Use piece L to make the top of the fuselage. Mountain fold in half horizontally. Then, on each side, measure and valley fold to form piece, as shown. Cut a 1 in (2.5 cm) slit along center crease at narrow end.

STEP 22 Use piece M to make a spar (support) for the wings. Valley fold in half vertically. Unfold. Mountain fold in half horizontally. Unfold. Then valley fold vertically so that outer edge meets center crease. Fold over again along original vertical center crease.

69

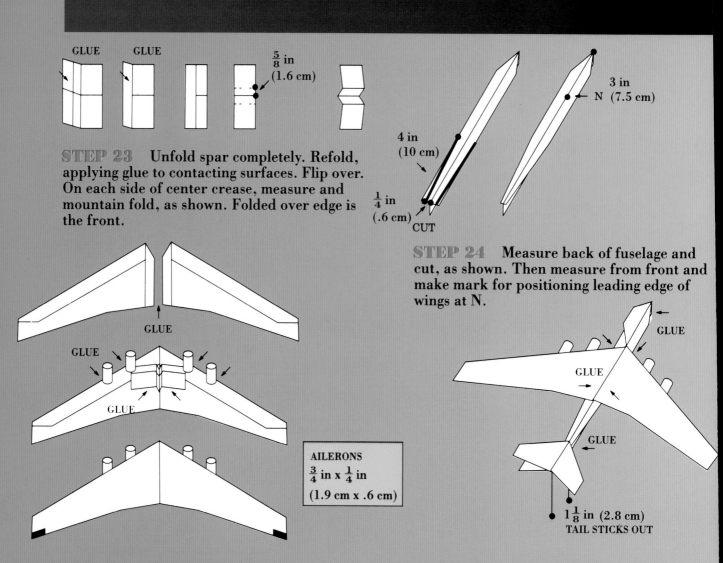

GLUE   GLUE

$\frac{5}{8}$ in
(1.6 cm)

4 in
(10 cm)

$\frac{1}{4}$ in
(.6 cm) CUT

3 in
N (7.5 cm)

STEP 23 Unfold spar completely. Refold, applying glue to contacting surfaces. Flip over. On each side of center crease, measure and mountain fold, as shown. Folded over edge is the front.

STEP 24 Measure back of fuselage and cut, as shown. Then measure from front and make mark for positioning leading edge of wings at **N**.

GLUE

GLUE

GLUE

GLUE

GLUE

GLUE

GLUE

AILERONS
$\frac{3}{4}$ in x $\frac{1}{4}$ in
(1.9 cm x .6 cm)

$1\frac{1}{8}$ in (2.8 cm)
TAIL STICKS OUT

STEP 25 With wings upside down, glue halves together. Glue spar to wings. Glue engines to wings in approximate positions shown (they stick out $\frac{1}{2}$ in (1.3 cm). Flip over. On trailing edges, make ailerons.

STEP 26 Apply glue to inside of fuselage, the small triangles on the bottom of canopy, and the center bottom of wings. Slide canopy tabs into fuselage aligning with front tip. Immediately slide wings in place. Then apply glue and slide tail into back of fuselage. Hold until glue sets.

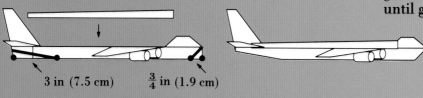

3 in (7.5 cm) $\frac{3}{4}$ in (1.9 cm)

BACK VIEW

STEP 27 Measure and cut nose and tail ends diagonally along heavy lines, as shown. Glue L onto top of fuselage, as shown, fitting snuggly against back of canopy, with vertical tail through the slit. Adjust dihedral (upward slanting of wings and tail), as shown.

FSW Concept

HISTORICAL INFORMATION

Airplane builders are always trying to make planes that are more suited to special tasks. In the 1980s a new shape of airplane appeared. Grumman introduced the X29 forward swept wing (FSW) experimental airplane, using new composite materials that were very light and strong. Such a design was impossible to build with traditional materials. The advantages of sweeping the wings forward instead of backward allow for maneuverability and high angle of attack flight — desirable qualities for military application. This paper airplane is modeled on a forward swept wing aircraft that has not yet been built. This concept, designed by Grumman, is being considered for possible future development.

Technical Information

A future fighter will have to operate over a wide range of speeds, be very maneuverable, and be fuel efficient. It will have to be able to land in very small spaces. Forward swept wings combined with strakes (extensions of the leading edges near the fuselage) will improve the flight characteristics of the plane at very low and very high speeds. However, having no horizontal tail makes the plane sensitive to correct balance, and computers will aid in control. The light weight of composites, the lack of a horizontal tail, and better engines will allow improved fuel efficiency. The FSW Concept will probably have two turbojet engines and be able to fly at more than twice the speed of sound at high altitudes. Its air intakes will be part of the large strakes. The plane will have a missile rail at each wingtip, and be able to carry extra fuel tanks and a variety of armament under the wings. Like present day fighters, this craft will be used for both air-to-air and air-to-ground operations. Besides its military role, this airplane could be a good candidate for aerial display at air shows.

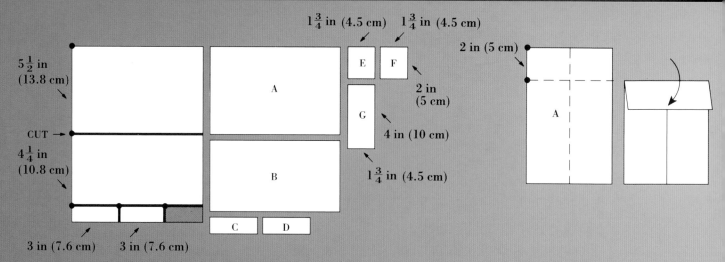

STEP 1   Measure and cut pieces from a sheet of bond paper. Three additional pieces, E, F, and G are needed, as shown.

STEP 2   To make the fuselage, lay piece A in a vertical direction. Fold in half vertically, using a valley fold. Unfold. Measure from top and valley fold, as shown.

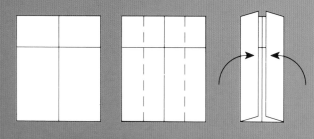

STEP 3   Valley fold each side so that outer edges meet center crease, as shown.

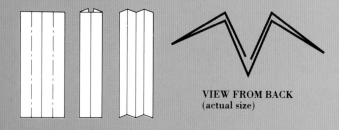

VIEW FROM BACK
(actual size)

STEP 4   Fold each side again using a mountain fold, so that outer edges meet center crease at back. Then adjust folds so that paper looks like an upside-down W, as shown.

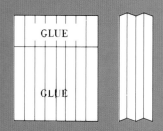

STEP 5   Unfold fuselage completely. Refold applying glue to all contacting surfaces, as shown. Make sure fuselage is straight.

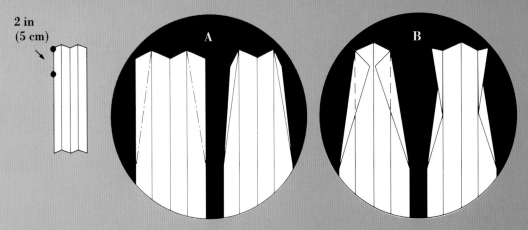

2 in (5 cm)

A

B

STEP 6 On each side, measure from top (front of fuselage), mark, and mountain fold along broken lines, as shown in enlarged view A. Then flip over fuselage. On each side, valley fold triangle along broken lines, matching fold line to existing crease, as shown in enlarged view B.

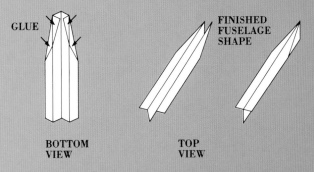

GLUE

FINISHED
FUSELAGE
SHAPE

BOTTOM
VIEW

TOP
VIEW

STEP 7 Glue triangles. Hold in place until glue sets. It is important that the fuselage stays straight. Do not glue nose yet.

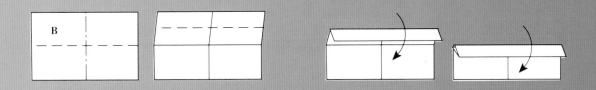

B

STEP 8 Use piece B to make the wings. Lay paper in a horizontal direction and fold in half vertically, using a mountain fold. Unfold. Valley fold in half horizontally. Unfold. Then valley fold horizontally so that top edge meets center crease. Fold over again along original center crease.

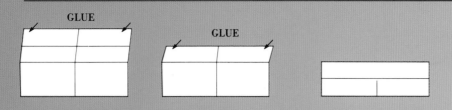

GLUE

GLUE

STEP 9   Unfold completely. Refold, applying glue to no more than 1 in (2.5 cm) from outer tips, as shown. The folded over part is the bottom of the leading edge (front) of the wings.

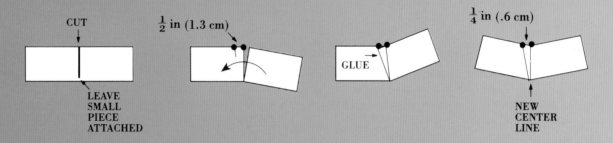

CUT

$\frac{1}{2}$ in (1.3 cm)

$\frac{1}{4}$ in (.6 cm)

GLUE

LEAVE
SMALL
PIECE
ATTACHED

NEW
CENTER
LINE

STEP 10   To sweep wings forward, cut along center line from the leading edge, leaving a small piece attached at the trailing edge (back). Then measure and make a mark on leading edge, as shown. Align pieces to the mark. Glue. Measure and draw new center line.

AILERONS $\frac{1}{2}$ in x $\frac{1}{4}$ in (1.3 cm x .6 cm)	ELEVATORS 1 in x $\frac{3}{8}$ in (2.5 cm x 1 cm)

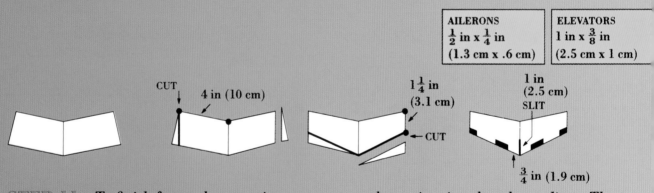

CUT   4 in (10 cm)

$1\frac{1}{4}$ in (3.1 cm)

1 in (2.5 cm) SLIT

← CUT

$\frac{3}{4}$ in (1.9 cm)

STEP 11   To finish forward swept wings, measure and cut wing tips along heavy lines. Then cut trailing edge along heavy lines, as shown. On trailing edges (back), make ailerons and elevators. From trailing edge, make a slit along center line, as shown.

RUDDERS 1 in x $\frac{3}{8}$ in (2.5 cm x 1 cm)

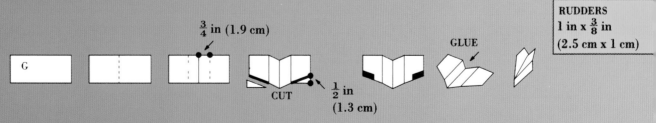

$\frac{3}{4}$ in (1.9 cm)

G

GLUE

CUT $\frac{1}{2}$ in (1.3 cm)

STEP 12   Use piece G to make the twin vertical tails. Lay paper in a horizontal direction. Valley fold in half vertically. Unfold. On each side, measure from center crease and mountain fold, as shown. Then measure and cut trailing edges, as shown by heavy lines. Make rudders. Glue center.

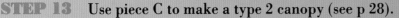

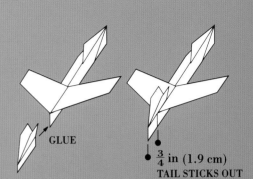

CANOPY (type 2)
$1\frac{1}{4}$ in x 3 in (3.1 cm x 7.5 cm)
Top point $1\frac{3}{4}$ in (4.5 cm)

STEP 13   Use piece C to make a type 2 canopy (see p 28).

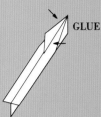

GLUE

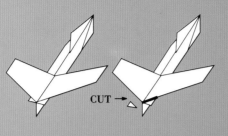

CUT →

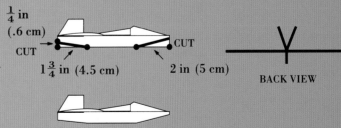

GLUE

$\frac{3}{4}$ in (1.9 cm)
TAIL STICKS OUT

STEP 14   Apply glue to inside of nose and the small triangular tabs on the bottom of canopy. Slide tabs into fuselage, aligning canopy with the tip of the nose. Hold until glue sets.

STEP 15   Glue wings in place, aligning at the trailing (back) edge. Make sure they are centered and at right angles to the fuselage. Trim fuselage back flush with the wing trailing (back) edges.

STEP 16   Measure and mark along bottom of tail. Apply glue and slide tail into back of fuselage (and slit in the wings) to the mark.

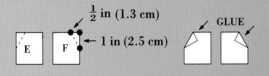

$\frac{1}{2}$ in (1.3 cm)

← 1 in (2.5 cm)

E   F

GLUE

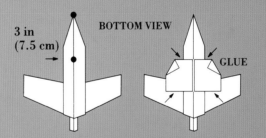

3 in (7.5 cm)

BOTTOM VIEW

GLUE

STEP 17   Use pieces E and F to make the strakes. Lay pieces vertically side by side, as shown. Measure on outer left and right edges and valley fold diagonally, as shown. Glue.

STEP 18   Turn airplane over. Measure from front and mark, as shown. On each side, glue strakes in place, aligning inside corners to the mark.

$\frac{3}{8}$ in (1 cm)

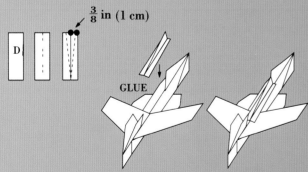

D

GLUE

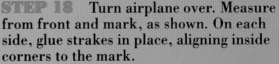

$\frac{1}{4}$ in (.6 cm)

CUT

$1\frac{3}{4}$ in (4.5 cm)

CUT

2 in (5 cm)

BACK VIEW

STEP 19   Lay piece D in a vertical direction to make the fuselage top. Mountain fold in half vertically. Unfold. On each side, measure and valley fold. Adjust shape, as shown. Glue onto top of fuselage, as shown, fitting the front snuggly over back of canopy.

STEP 20   Measure and cut nose and tail diagonally, as shown by heavy lines. This plane has no dihedral. Twin tails are canted (tilted), as shown.

SST Concept

HISTORICAL INFORMATION

Flying faster than the speed of sound can only be done in areas of the world where no people live, because the loud sonic boom would break the windows in people's houses. Therefore, supersonic flights are undertaken only between cities across the world's oceans. However, the Sukoi and Gulfstream airplane companies are experimenting with planes of different shapes and sizes to see if they can reduce the intensity of the sonic boom. If the boom can be made quieter, supersonic air service between cities on the same continent or even in the same country would be possible. This paper airplane is modeled on a plane that has not yet been built. It is a concept of a future supersonic transport plane (SST).

Technical Information

The type of airplane being planned is probably small, carrying no more than ten passengers. This small size would be one way of making the boom produced in supersonic flight less damaging. The goal is to make the plane capable of traveling nearly twice the speed of sound. It will probably be built of lightweight composite materials and use computers for flight control. The plane's main wings will be delta wings with winglets at the tips. Winglets help direct the airflow over the wings. Canard wings for added control will also be used. This plane might be the business jet of the future.

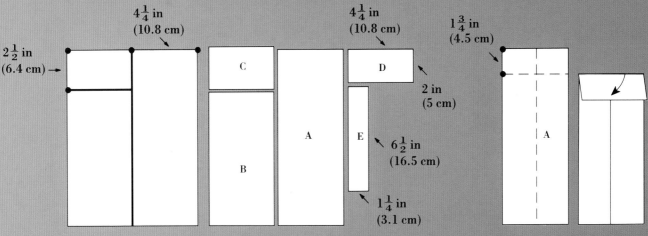

STEP 1 Measure and cut the various pieces from a sheet of bond paper. Two additional pieces, D and E, are needed, as shown.

STEP 2 To make the fuselage, fold piece A in half vertically using a valley fold. Unfold. Measure from top and valley fold, as shown.

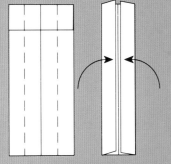

STEP 3 Valley fold each side so that outer edges meet center crease, as shown.

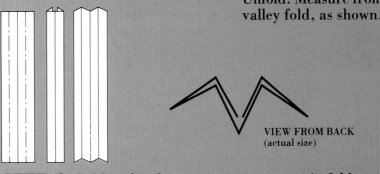

VIEW FROM BACK
(actual size)

STEP 4 Fold each side again using a mountain fold, so that outer edges meet center crease at back. Then adjust folds so that paper looks like an upside-down W, as shown.

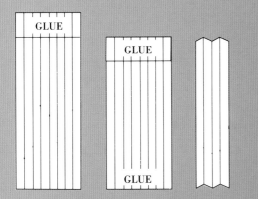

STEP 5 Unfold fuselage completely. Refold applying glue to contacting surfaces, as shown. Make sure fuselage is straight.

$4\frac{1}{8}$ in
(10.5 cm)

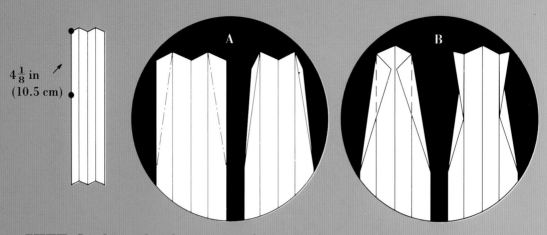

A B

STEP 6 On each side, measure from top (front of fuselage), mark, and mountain fold along broken lines, as shown in enlarged view A. Then flip over fuselage. On each side, valley fold triangle along broken lines, matching fold line to existing crease, as shown in enlarged view B.

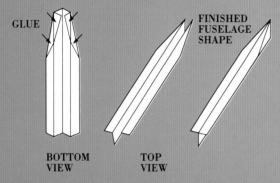

GLUE

FINISHED
FUSELAGE
SHAPE

BOTTOM
VIEW

TOP
VIEW

STEP 7 Glue triangles. Hold in place until glue sets. It is important that the fuselage stays straight. Do not glue nose yet.

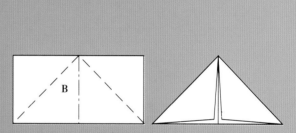

B

STEP 8 Lay piece B flat in a horizontal direction to make the wings. Fold in half vertically, using a mountain fold. Unfold. On each side, valley fold diagonally so that top edge meets center crease, as shown.

GLUE

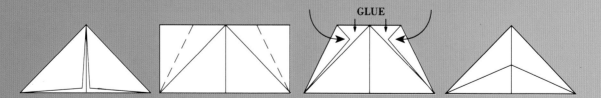

STEP 9 Unfold diagonal folds. On each side, valley fold diagonally so that outer edges meet diagonal crease, as shown. Apply glue to small upper triangles only and refold original diagonal creases.

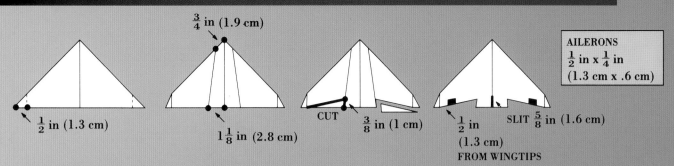

$\frac{3}{4}$ in (1.9 cm)

$\frac{1}{2}$ in (1.3 cm)

$1\frac{1}{8}$ in (2.8 cm)

CUT

$\frac{3}{8}$ in (1 cm)

$\frac{1}{2}$ in (1.3 cm)

SLIT $\frac{5}{8}$ in (1.6 cm)

FROM WINGTIPS

STEP 10 Flip wings over. To make winglets, measure at each wingtip and valley fold, as shown. Then on each side, measure and draw lines, as shown. At the trailing edge, measure and cut, as shown by heavy lines. Make ailerons in locations shown. Measure and cut a slit in location shown.

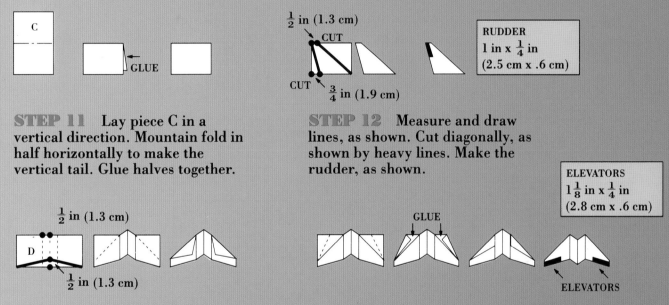

C

GLUE

$\frac{1}{2}$ in (1.3 cm)

CUT

CUT $\frac{3}{4}$ in (1.9 cm)

STEP 11 Lay piece C in a vertical direction. Mountain fold in half horizontally to make the vertical tail. Glue halves together.

STEP 12 Measure and draw lines, as shown. Cut diagonally, as shown by heavy lines. Make the rudder, as shown.

$\frac{1}{2}$ in (1.3 cm)

D

$\frac{1}{2}$ in (1.3 cm)

GLUE

ELEVATORS

STEP 13 Lay piece D in a horizontal direction to make canard wings. Mountain fold in half vertically. Unfold. Measure from bottom along center crease and cut, as shown by heavy lines. On each side, measure and valley fold. Then on each side, fold diagonally so that top edge meets vertical crease.

STEP 14 Unfold diagonal folds. On each side, valley fold diagonally so that outer edges meet diagonal creases, as shown. Apply glue to small upper triangles only and refold original diagonal creases. Flip wings over and make elevators in locations shown.

SLIT $\frac{5}{8}$ in (1.6 cm)

E

STEP 15 Use piece E to make a type 1 canopy (see p 28).

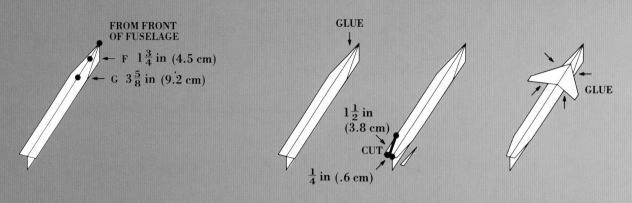

FROM FRONT OF FUSELAGE

F $1\frac{3}{4}$ in (4.5 cm)

G $3\frac{5}{8}$ in (9.2 cm)

GLUE

$1\frac{1}{2}$ in (3.8 cm)

CUT

$\frac{1}{4}$ in (.6 cm)

GLUE

STEP 16   Measure from front of fuselage and make marks for positioning the leading edges of canard wings and canopy at F and main wings at G, as shown.

STEP 17   Apply glue to inside of nose, no more than 1 in (2.5 cm) from tip. Hold until glue sets. Then measure and cut back of fuselage, as shown. Glue canard wings in place. (Do not glue the inside center of the canard wings.)

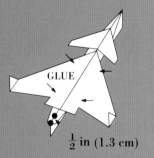

GLUE

$\frac{1}{2}$ in (1.3 cm)

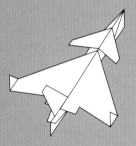

STEP 18   Glue main wings in place, making sure they are centered and at right angles to the fuselage. Then measure from back of fuselage and mark.

STEP 19   Apply glue and slide vertical tail into back of fuselage so that trailing edge aligns with mark.

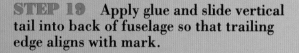

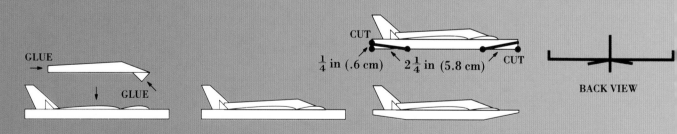

GLUE

GLUE

CUT

$\frac{1}{4}$ in (.6 cm) $2\frac{1}{4}$ in (5.8 cm)   CUT

BACK VIEW

STEP 20   Apply glue to the tabs on the bottom of canopy and the inside back of the canopy. Slide tab into center of canard wings with the slit fitting around the vertical tail. Align canopy front with front of canard wings.

STEP 21   Measure and cut nose and tail, as shown by heavy lines. The wings of this airplane have no dihedral. Adjust winglets to a vertical position.

TAV Concept

HISTORICAL INFORMATION

We are living on the threshold of a new era in air travel. Already the space shuttle is blasting into space attached to a rocket and returning as an airplane for another mission. The next generation of space planes will take off under their own power from ordinary airport runways, fly into space, and return back to earth. They are called trans-atmospheric vehicles (TAV). Sometimes they are called hypersonic transports (HST). They will combine jet and rocket engines for propulsion and have stable delta wings (triangle shaped) integrated into the fuselage for lift in the lower atmosphere. They will look something like the ordinary "paper plane." One example is NASAs experimental X30. This paper airplane is modeled on such future space planes.

Technical Information

Trans-atmospheric vehicles will need powerful and complicated engines and fuel supplies if they are to fly from the ground up into space. It takes a great deal of energy to propel an airplane beyond the limits of the earth's atmosphere and go into space orbit at 22 times the speed of sound. For example, the space shuttle we have now uses over 1,000,000 lb (600,000 kg) of liquid oxygen and 300,000 lb (120,000 kg) of liquid hydrogen, which it burns in under ten minutes of flight. The fuel is carried in large external tanks, which are thrown away during each flight. Future TAVs will carry everything on-board, like a regular airplane. In addition to engines for very high altitude, they will also have engines that can burn fuel using oxygen from the atmosphere at lower altitudes. Only at very high altitudes, where there is not enough oxygen in the air to use, will they switch to an on-board supply of oxygen. Space planes of the future will use less fuel and carry much less oxygen. Such planes will be able to fly competely around the world in just a few hours.

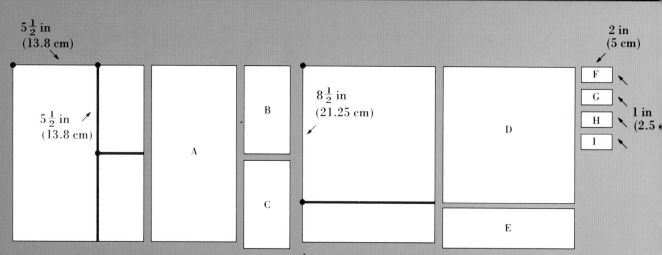

STEP 1 Measure and cut the various pieces from two sheets of bond paper. Four additional small pieces are needed, as shown.

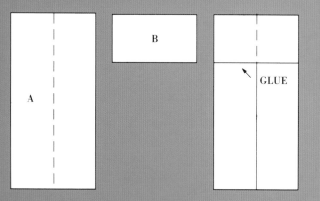

STEP 2 Lay piece A flat in a vertical direction. To make the fuselage, fold in half vertically using a valley fold. Unfold. To make nose ballast glue piece B in place, aligning the top edges, as shown. Refold center crease. Unfold again.

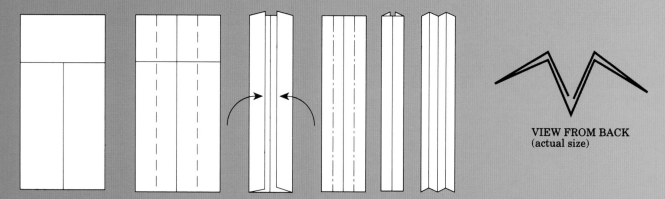

STEP 3 Refold in half vertically using a valley fold. Unfold. Valley fold each side so that outer edges meet center crease, as shown. Fold each side again using a mountain fold, so that outer edges meet center crease at back. Then adjust folds so that paper looks like an upside-down W, as shown.

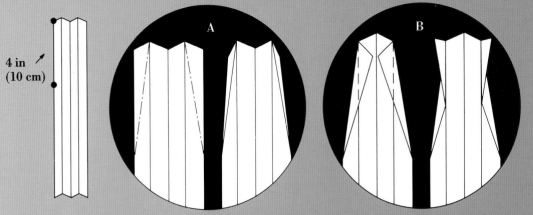

4 in
(10 cm)

STEP 4 On each side, measure from top (front of fuselage), mark, and mountain fold along broken lines, as shown in enlarged view A. Then flip over fuselage. On each side, valley fold the triangle along the broken lines, matching fold line to existing crease, as shown in enlarged view B.

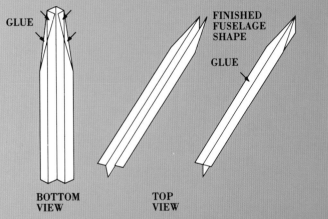

GLUE

BOTTOM
VIEW

TOP
VIEW

FINISHED
FUSELAGE
SHAPE

GLUE

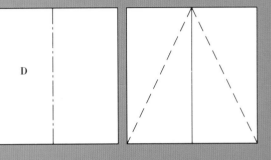

D

STEP 5 Glue triangles. Hold in place until glue sets. It is important that the fuselage stays straight. Glue fuselage in the middle only, leaving the nose and tail ends unglued.

STEP 6 Use piece D to make the wings. Mountain fold in half vertically. Unfold. Then on each side valley fold diagonally along a line running from the top center to the bottom corners. Unfold.

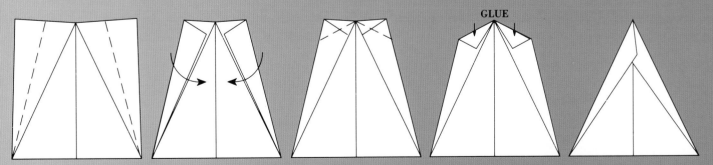

GLUE

STEP 7 On each side, valley fold diagonally so that outer edges meet diagonal crease, as shown. Then fold so that upper edges meet diagonal crease, as shown. Apply glue to the small upper triangles only and refold original diagonal creases.

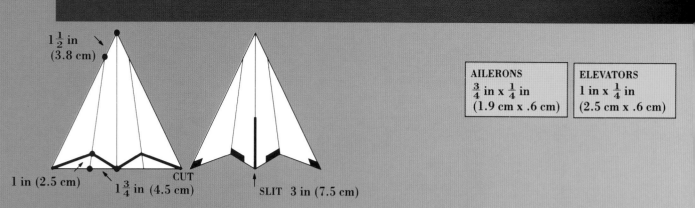

AILERONS
$\frac{3}{4}$ in x $\frac{1}{4}$ in
(1.9 cm x .6 cm)

ELEVATORS
1 in x $\frac{1}{4}$ in
(2.5 cm x .6 cm)

$1\frac{1}{2}$ in
(3.8 cm)

1 in (2.5 cm)

$1\frac{3}{4}$ in (4.5 cm)

CUT

SLIT   3 in (7.5 cm)

STEP 8   Lay wings flat right side up. On each side measure from front tip and back center and draw lines, as shown. Then cut wings, as shown by heavy lines. Make elevators and ailerons in locations shown. At the trailing (back) edge, cut a slit along center crease, as shown.

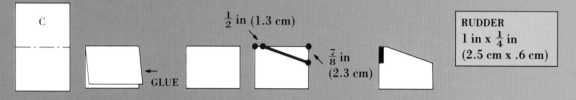

C

$\frac{1}{2}$ in (1.3 cm)

$\frac{7}{8}$ in (2.3 cm)

GLUE

RUDDER
1 in x $\frac{1}{4}$ in
(2.5 cm x .6 cm)

STEP 9   Mountain fold piece C in half horizontally to make the vertical tail. Glue halves together. Measure and cut, as shown by heavy line. Make rudder, as shown.

CANOPY (type 1)
3 in x $8\frac{1}{2}$ in (7.8 cm x 21.25 cm)
Top point 3 in (7.8 cm)
Front $\frac{3}{4}$ in (1.9 cm)

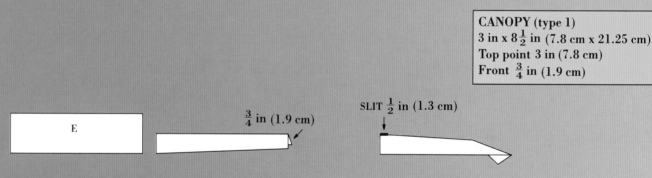

E

$\frac{3}{4}$ in (1.9 cm)

SLIT $\frac{1}{2}$ in (1.3 cm)

STEP 10   Use piece E to make the type 1 canopy (see p 28). Note that this canopy is lower at the front than at the back. Cut paper to size first.

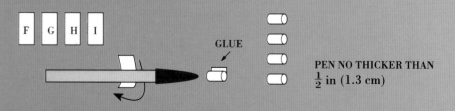

F   G   H   I

GLUE

PEN NO THICKER THAN
$\frac{1}{2}$ in (1.3 cm)

STEP 11   Use pieces F, G, H, and I to make the engines. Wrap paper around a felt pen vertically and glue.

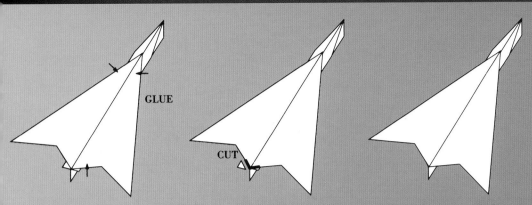

STEP 12 Glue wings to the fuselage, aligning trailing (back) edges. Make sure wings are centered and at right angles to the fuselage. Then trim back of fuselage to match wing trailing edges.

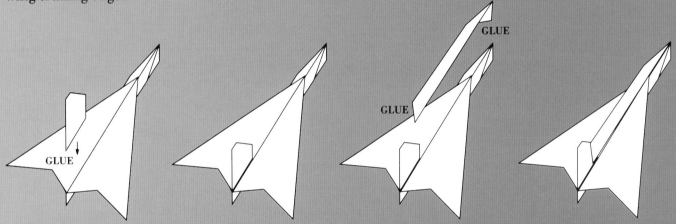

STEP 13 Apply glue and slide vertical tail into fuselage (and the slit in the wings). Align at trailing (back) edges. Apply glue to the lower front tab of the canopy and the inside back. Position canopy by inserting tab into nose end of the fuselage and slipping the back over the vertical tail.

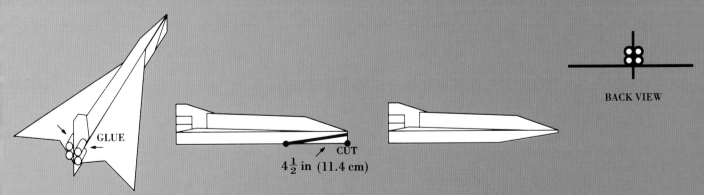

BACK VIEW

4½ in (11.4 cm)

STEP 14 Attach the engines by gluing them to the vertical tail, two on each side, one on top the other, as shown. Align to the trailing edge of the vertical tail.

STEP 15 Measure and cut nose diagonally, as shown by heavy line. This plane has no dihedral.

Decoration

The following pages contain a plan (top) view and an elevation (side) view of each of the paper airplanes contained in this book. They have window outlines, outlines of control surfaces, and other lines that help define each plane's shape, all of which add to an airplane's realism. Decorative patterns add interest.

The patterns can be copied, modified, or you can invent your own. A pattern such as a checkerboard or a camouflage that is shown on one plane can easily be applied to another airplane design. Use your imagination. What you see here are suggestions. Or you can build paper airplanes and leave them undecorated. You may wish to build undecorated trial planes first so you can master their construction and flight before you spend a lot of time on decoration.

It is easier to add decoration to the airplanes before they are completely assembled. Some advanced planning is needed. Once you have decided on the pattern or design you want for the plane, decorate the pieces as you cut and fold them. Try each piece for fit and mark it carefully as you go along. Armament can be added to military planes using toothpicks. Draw the decoration lines using a very fine black felt-tipped pen. Narrow colored markers are ideal for filling in. Avoid water-based markers because they wrinkle the paper too much. Stencils can be used to add numbers and letters.

See the photographed airplanes for ideas on color schemes. Some of the patterns may be different from those shown here.

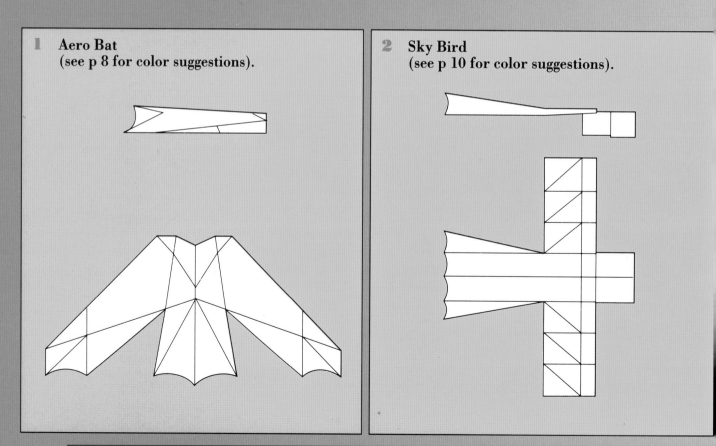

1 **Aero Bat**
(see p 8 for color suggestions).

2 **Sky Bird**
(see p 10 for color suggestions).

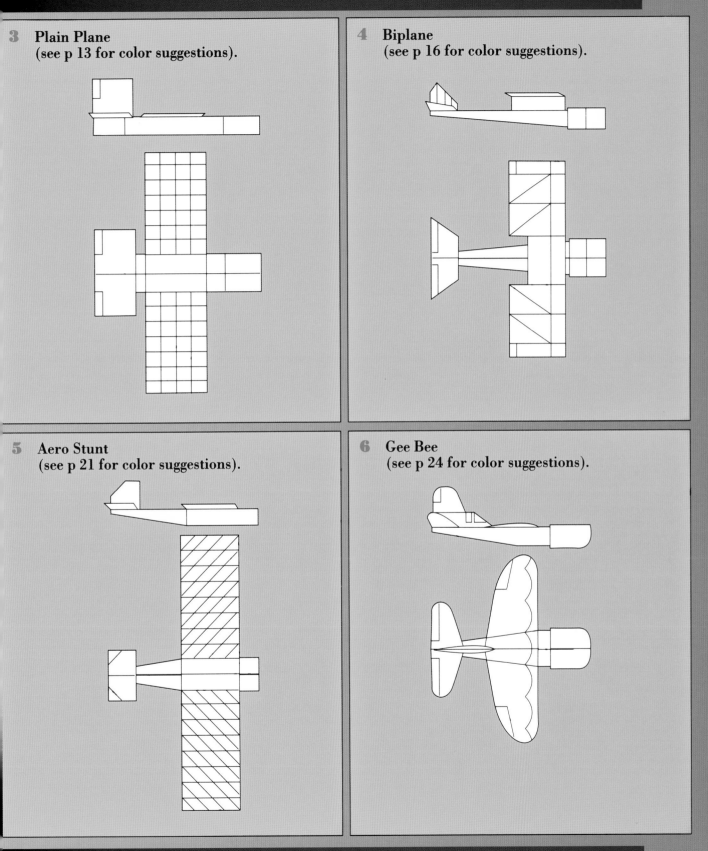

3 **Plain Plane**
(see p 13 for color suggestions).

4 **Biplane**
(see p 16 for color suggestions).

5 **Aero Stunt**
(see p 21 for color suggestions).

6 **Gee Bee**
(see p 24 for color suggestions).

7 **P47 Thunderbolt**
(see p 29 for color suggestions).

8 **DH108 Swallow**
(see p 33 for color suggestions).

9 **X1**
(see p 37 for color suggestions).

10 **Mirage 2000**
(see p 42 for color suggestions).

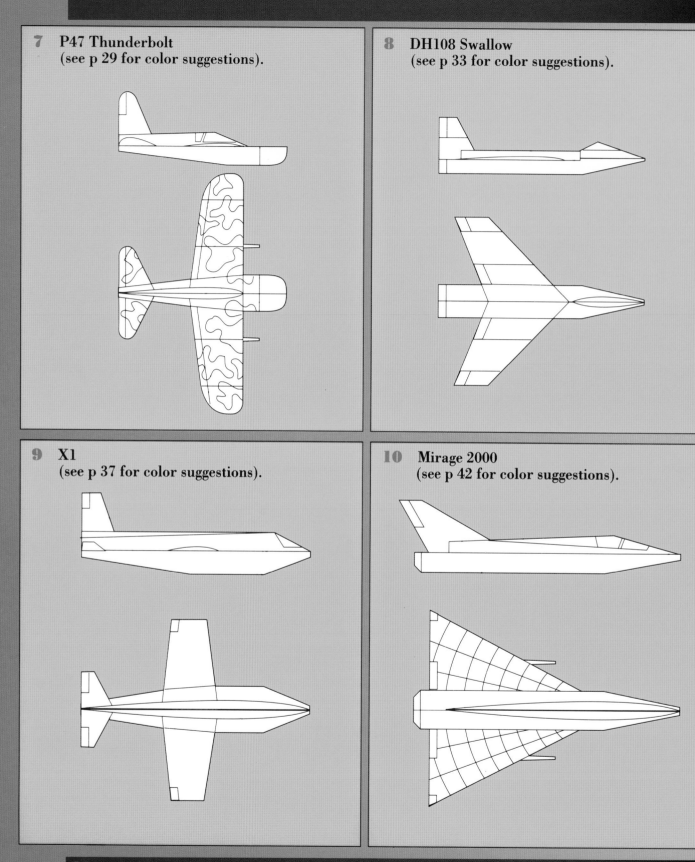

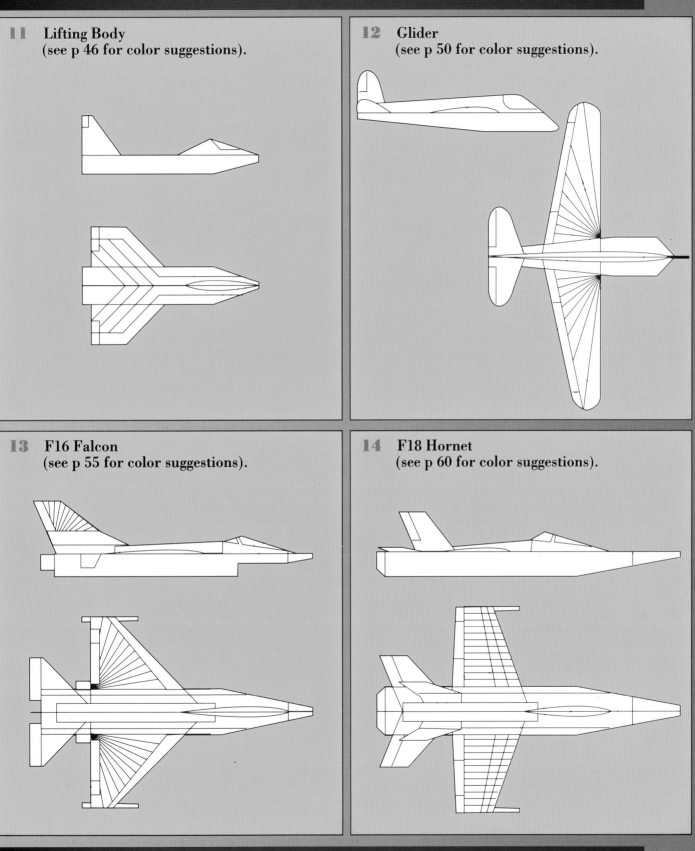

11 Lifting Body
(see p 46 for color suggestions).

12 Glider
(see p 50 for color suggestions).

13 F16 Falcon
(see p 55 for color suggestions).

14 F18 Hornet
(see p 60 for color suggestions).

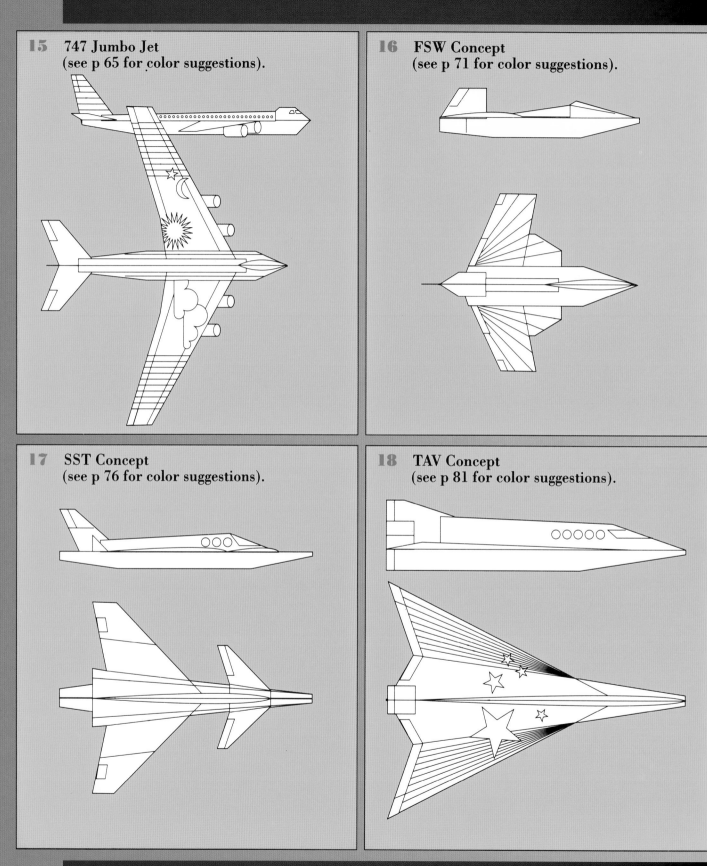

15 747 Jumbo Jet
(see p 65 for color suggestions).

16 FSW Concept
(see p 71 for color suggestions).

17 SST Concept
(see p 76 for color suggestions).

18 TAV Concept
(see p 81 for color suggestions).

Glossary

Angle of attack The downward slant, from front to back, of a wing.

Angle of bank The raising of the outside wing and lowering of the inside wing during a turn.

Aspect ratio The length of a wing in relation to its width. The longer a wing, the higher its aspect ratio.

Attitude The direction an airplane is pointing in relation to the horizon (banking, yawing, or pitching).

Ballast Extra weight needed in the nose of an airplane to make the center of gravity coincide with the wings, which provide the lift.

Control surfaces Small surfaces that can be bent to alter the airflow and change an airplane's attitude — ailerons for bank, elevators for pitch, and rudders for yaw.

Dihedral angle Upward slanting of wings away from the fuselage. (Downward slanting is called anhedral.)

Drag The resistance of air on moving objects, slowing them down.

Fuselage The body of an airplane.

Leading edges The front edges of wings, tails, or other parts.

Lift The force of air pressure beneath the wings buoying up an airplane.

Maneuver Skilfully making an airplane fly in a desired direction — turn, climb, dive, stall, spin, or loop.

Pitch Nose up or nose down attitude.

Roll Rotation along the length of an airplane.

Spar The main internal frame that supports the wing.

Strakes Wedge-shaped extensions of the wing's leading (front) edges near the fuselage.

Trailing edges The back edges of wings, tails, or other parts.

Trim Making small adjustments to the control surfaces to affect the attitude of an airplane.

Trim drag The drag (resistance) produced from bending control surfaces into the airflow.

Ventral fin A small stabilizer on each side of the fuselage underneath the tail.

Wing loading The amount of weight a given area of wing is required to lift.

Yaw Nose left or nose right attitude.

Flying Tips

Don't be discouraged if on first flight your paper airplane "corkscrews" and crashes. Flying paper airplanes is a delicate balancing act. Only when everything works in harmony – wings, horizontal tail, vertical tail, and control surfaces – is successful flight achieved. With each paper airplane that you build, aim to improve the construction. When carefully made and trimmed, the paper airplanes in this book are super flyers. But remember, the performance of each airplane differs. Experimentation is necessary in order to achieve maximum performance. This is part of the fun of flying paper planes.

Folds that are not neat and crisp add drag to the airplane. This will decrease glide performance. Sloppy folds can also result in twisted airplanes. Inaccurate gluing does not help matters. A twisted plane is sure to "corkscrew" badly (see p 7). The importance of careful folds cannot be over emphasized.

Airplanes must be symmetrical – one side must be just like the other. On both sides wing and horizontal tail sizes, shapes, and thicknesses must be the same. Also make sure that the control surfaces on one side are the same sizes and are bent the same amount as on the other side.

Make sure that the dihedral (upward slanting of wings and tail) is adjusted correctly. In each design, refer to the last step of construction for suggestions. Sometimes experimentation with different dihedral (or none at all) will be successful. Dihedral povides stability, however, too much dihedral has a destabilizing effect.

Some of the airplanes in this book have secondary control surfaces(flaps). Secondary control surfaces need special mention. If they are bent down slightly, lift is increased. If they are bent down 90° drag is greatly increased and the nose will pitch down. Additional up elevator is needed, increasing the angle of attack but also increasing drag. Trimmed in this way an airplane does not glide very far. In full-sized airplanes, this trim is good for landing. Experiment with different settings of the secondary control surfaces. Adjust carefully for best results.

Paper airplanes are not baseballs. They cannot be thrown hard. To launch, hold the fuselage lightly between thumb and forefinger near the point where the plane balances. Throw with a firm forward motion keeping the nose level, pushing the airplane more than throwing it. With a bit of practice you will discover just how hard each of the planes need to be thrown under different conditions.

Pitch trim Although the paper airplanes in this book are built to resemble powered aircraft, they are obviously all gliders. For thrust they must convert altitude into airspeed (see p 10). The pitching axis is very important in determining airspeed. Once properly trimmed, an airplane will always fly at the same speed. If the airplane zooms toward the ground, bend the elevators up slightly to raise the nose. If more speed is needed, as in outdoor flight, less up elevator will produce the desired result.

Roll trim Providing the wings are not twisted, the wings should remain more or less level in flight. If one wing drops, bend the aileron on that wing down slightly and up slightly on the other wing.

Yaw trim If the plane still has a tendency to turn, bend the rudder slightly opposite to the direction of the turn.

For additional information about trimming see
pages 13, 16, and 21.

Further Reading

Boyne, Walter. *The Leading Edge*. Stewart,
Tabori & Chang, New York, 1986.

Mackie, Dan. *Flight*. Hayes, Burlington, 1986.

Schmidt, Norman. *Discover Aerodynamics With
Paper Airplanes*. Peguis, Winnipeg, 1991.

Schmidt, Norman. *Best Ever Paper Airplanes*.
Sterling/Tamos, New York, 1994.

Taylor, Michael. *History of Flight*. Crescent,
New York, 1990.

Index